THE QUEST FOR
THE DIVINE STICKY STUFF
20 short plays for churches

Chris Chapman, Susan Chapman, Peter Gregory and Heather Allison

The Joint Board of Christian Education
Melbourne

Published by
THE JOINT BOARD OF CHRISTIAN EDUCATION
Second Floor, 10 Queen Street, Melbourne 3000, Australia.

For commercial performance permission, write to
Chris and Sue Chapman, 54 Premier Street, Oxley, Queensland 4075, Australia.

National Library of Australia
  Cataloguing-in-Publication entry.

  The quest for the divine sticky stuff.

    ISBN 0 85819 790 1.

    1. Christian drama, Australian. 2. Young adult drama, Australian. I. Chapman, Chris, 1957-
    II. Joint Board of Christian Education.

A822.05160809283

First printed 1990
Reprinted 1993

Cover and cover design: Kelvin Young
Design: Pat Baker
Typeset: on Ventura Publisher in Zapf Calligraphic by JBCE
Printer: Lutheran Publishing House

JB93/3377

CONTENTS

INTRODUCTION

These plays have been written to be used in a wide variety of situations—of which full stage production is only one option. They are also eminently suitable for readings, quick sketch formats, fellowship discussion groups and so on. Therefore, a group wishing to stage one or more of the dramas need not be put off by lists of props, stage directions, light and sound effects as, in virtually all cases, easy alternatives are available.

Blackouts and curtains, for instance, can be replaced by a posture freeze on the last line, followed by a snappy exit to the thunderous applause which will, of course, occur. A simple stage exit can often achieve the same effect. It would become tedious to list all the alternative possibilities for each play. Just look at what you have available and take it from there. The production of any of these plays comes well within the reach of the average youth fellowship or young adult group with a few chairs, a table, and a bit of imagination.

Some of the plays contain references to particular persons or events that were topical or contemporary at the time of writing. Other names and references may be substituted. This also applies to local references, e.g. you may change the rugby terms to those applicable to another football code if this is more appropriate in your setting.

Many of the characters can be either male or female, depending on the people available to play the roles. Just remember to change the "he", "she", "him" and "her" references where necessary.

ACKNOWLEDGMENTS

The production of this book could never have become a reality without the tireless assistance of many friends, pots of tea, Heather's scone-ring, and the wonders of an Apple 2e. The dramas could never have been written in the first place without the prompting and guidance supplied generously (even in the most difficult moments and the latest of hours) by the ultimate communicator and comedian—the Holy Spirit.

THE QUEST FOR THE DIVINE STICKY STUFF

CHARACTERS

Voice off
Saul
Solomon
Rebecca
Ruth
Shadrach
Dorcas
St Peter

Part 1

SCENE:	*Curtain opens to reveal Saul and Solomon, rather doddery and senile, sitting in comfy arm and rocking chairs, reading newspapers, drinking tea, etc. If no curtain, the two characters can dodder in and sit.*
Voice off:	Another dreary afternoon at the Evenpsalm Old Testament Senior Citizens Home. The air is filled with the soothing sounds of Denture Cleanse fizzing in denture glasses, the clink of ceremonial seven branched bedpans, and a belch, a wheeze and a whisper.
Rebecca:	*(Offstage.)* Give us a kiss, sonny.
Voice off:	And it's with a belch, a wheeze and a whisper that we get on into our story.
Saul:	Solomon, are you going to sit there all day and do nothing again?
Solomon:	Er, yes. What are you going to do, Saul?
Saul:	King Saul, please.
Solomon:	Not if you don't call me King Solomon.
Saul:	Oh, all right. Anyway, after what you did to my kingdom after David died, you don't deserve to be called king.
Solomon:	Oh yeah. What about you, you old...
Rebecca:	*(Struggling on with walking stick.)* Oh dear, are you boys fighting again? Every time I turn my back you're at it again.
Solomon:	You shut your gums, Jezebel, you old bat.
Rebecca:	I'm not Jezebel, I'm Rebecca. Jezebel was the fat one who used to sell Crave-on beauty products.
Solomon:	Oh yes, you're Rebecca, Isaac's old lady.
Saul:	Yeah, Rebecca, this is man's talk. You butt out of it. You were worse than either of us. I've been reading all about you recently.

Solomon: Yeah. Hairy arms, eh? Goat skin coat, eh?

Saul: Yeah, tricking your old man like that.

Rebecca: You keep quiet. I'd do the same to you if I had half a chance. And what about your career? It wasn't exactly spotless so I'm led to believe.

Solomon: Yeah. Heh heh heh.

Saul: Nor was yours, kingy baby.

Solomon: Oh yeah. Well let's see what it says in the social pages about you, sonny. (Reads 1 Samuel 15:26-28.)

Saul: (Grabs Bible off him.) Well, you think that's bad? Gimme that. Let's see what it says about you. It says here you had 700 wives ... you stupid fellow.

Solomon: Oh, it had its good points.

Saul: Like what?

Solomon: Well, for one thing, we all took turns to do the washing up in our family, so I only did it twice in my whole life. But boy, was it a big one!

Rebecca: Male chauvinist!

Solomon: Aaah!

Rebecca: So what does it all go to prove?

Solomon: Well, I guess none of us did too well, eh?

Saul: I did okay for a while. Till I started doing things my own way. Really mucked it up when I went to see the Witch of Endor for the battle predictions after Samuel the prophet died. Boy, was she ever ugly, a real hag. I'll never forget her.

Rebecca: Is that so? Ha ha ha hee hee heeee.

Saul: I can see why I'll never forget her.

Solomon: Well, I started off nicely too—but all those women! They messed up my whole house.

Rebecca: Your house was a hole anyway. You can't blame women for everything.

Solomon: I can.

Rebecca: Well, I did all right most of the time, but I got dishonest and tricked the old man up. Then I wasn't so popular.

Saul: None of us stuck to the right way. We all started off right and devian ... devers ... detest ... moved off.

Solomon: Does that mean we didn't stick to our guns?

Saul: Of course we didn't stick to our guns. They weren't invented.

Solomon: Oh yes.

Rebecca: Well you can stick to your gums if you like, but I'd rather have removable dentures.

Solomon: Not gums, guns!

(Piano and drum patter to introduce new characters. See music on page 11. Use piano vamp and drums, drums only, or vocal ostinato as outlined. This fast beat patter accompanies the characters RUTH, SHADRACH and DORCAS as they come in, speak their rhythm lines, and move aside and off. If no instruments are available, the characters can make a rhythm with voice, hand clapping, finger snapping, etc.)

Rebecca: Oh no! It's Miss Success Story again. The lady who stuck to her family and friends. Yuk!

(RUTH enters and walks to centre stage. Two bars of ostinato to fit each line.)

Ruth: Hello everybody, my name is Ruth,
Everything I tell you is the honest truth.
I stayed with Naomi, my dear old ma,
Even though our journey took us off so far.
I stuck to my friends right from the start,
And won myself a husband with my kind warm heart.
Oh yeah.

(The oldies also now speak in time with the patter.)

Rebecca: I hope the others aren't coming too.

(SHADRACH enters.)

Oh dear, looky there. I spoke too soon.

Saul: And who are you? Tell us your name.

Shadrach: I'm Shadrach, the Jew of furnace fame.
They tried to get me to bow to their rules,
But me and my mates, we ain't no fools.
We stuck together and we stuck to the Lord,
So nothing couldn't hurt us, not fire nor sword.
Oh yeah.

Solomon: I wish you'd move and get out quick.
You goody goodies are making me sick.

Dorcas: If you're down and out and feeling hurt,
If you're cold and hungry and covered in dirt,
My name is Dorcas and I'm no flirt,
Come around to me and I'll sew you a shirt.
Oh yeah.

All: We are some goodies who you read about.
See for yourselves how our lives worked out.
Our stickability helped us in the fight.
We were always loyal and stuck to the right.
Oh yeah.

(SHADRACH, RUTH and DORCAS exeunt to patter.)

Solomon: *(Exploding.)* It's not fair! Everyone thinks that lot are so good because they stuck to the right way, and then we get the blame because we didn't.

Saul: I wanna be like Ruth.

Rebecca: Well we can't be like Ruth, because she's got it and we haven't.

Saul: I reckon there's some sort of personality trait that she got given when she was made that makes her better able to stick to things.

Rebecca: It's not fair. God should have given me more of the old stick.

Solomon: You are the old stick.

Rebecca: I think we should all have got more of that stuff whatever it is—that glue.

Solomon: The Divine Sticky Stuff.

Saul: That's what it is. The Divine Sticky Stuff. We must have it.

Rebecca: I say we go to the Pearly Gates and demand more Divine Sticky Stuff so we can be patient and enduring like those others.

(Music FX plays "Land of Hope and Glory" or similar stirring tune over.)

Saul: We shall search and search until we find it. Naught shall stop us.

Solomon: Gird up your walking frames for battle.

Rebecca: Knitting needles shall be beaten into swords and patchwork knee rugs into suits of shining armour. Onward, to the Pearly Gates!

(They all attempt to rise from their chairs but can't do so until REBECCA jabs SAUL in the backside with knitting needle and he jumps up and then gives the rest a hand. They all march off, waving walking sticks. CURTAIN/blackout.)

Voice off: We-ell, isn't that exciting? But there's more, folks, in the next episode of the Quest for the Divine Sticky Stuff. Part 2 coming up soon.

Part 2

Voice off: We proudly present the winners of this year's Up the Creek Stage Presentation Awards... Wait on... I apologise for that. It's not ... and ... *(Insert names of local youth group leaders, or similar.)* It's part 2 of The Quest for the Divine Sticky Stuff. Scene: The Pearly Gates, St Peter on guard.

(CURTAIN opens.)

Ruth: St Peter ... yoo hoo.

St Peter: Halt. Who goes there? If there's someone there, call out. If there's no one there, don't call out. *(Name of prominent politician or real estate agent)*, if that's you—go away. We ain't selling out!

Ruth: It's me, Ruth.

St Peter: Ah Ruth, come on over. Haven't seen you for a while.

Ruth: Er Peter, I think you are about to have some visitors.

St Peter:	Visitors? What visitors?
Ruth:	It's what's-their-names ... Saul, Solomon and Rebecca. I thought I'd better warn you. They've come to complain about not being good.
St Peter:	What's the point of complaining about that? There's nothing I can do. It's their own decision.
Ruth:	Oh, they think that I was given something that makes it easy for me to be good. They say that they've been disadvantaged.
St Peter:	The poor darlings. So I suppose it's all God's fault.
	(SOLOMON, SAUL and REBECCA enter. They could be carrying placards.)
Solomon:	There they are. The Pearly Gates and St Peter.
Rebecca:	Equal sticky stuff rights for all.
Solomon:	We want more sticky stuff.
Saul:	Twelve per cent rise in sticky stuff rates.
Rebecca:	With indexation to keep up with inflation.
St Peter:	Quiet down, please. Shhhhh!
Solomon:	Ruth got more of the Divine Sticky Stuff than we did and it's not fair.
Ruth:	That's not true.
Rebecca:	Then how come you stuck to your family and friends?
Saul:	And to the right way when we couldn't?
Ruth:	But that was my decision. I couldn't leave Naomi to fend for herself.
Rebecca:	No, we want more sticky stuff.
All three:	Yes, more sticky stuff for all. More sticky stuff.
St Peter:	Quiet. Quiet. Cease! Maybe you got some more of another talent to make up for it.
All three:	No! More sticky stuff. We want more sticky stuff.
Ruth:	You've got it all wrong. There's nothing special about me.
All three:	No! More sticky stuff, sticky stuff, we want sticky stuff.
	(General picket line rabble.)
St Peter:	Stop! Shut up!! Be quiet!!! Maybe it's still coming.
All three:	*(General hubbub.)*
St Peter:	Quiet. Quiet. Are you sure she got more than you did?
Ruth:	I didn't. That's not true.
All three:	Yes she did! Yes she did!
	(General racket from all three.)
St Peter:	All right, all right. I'll go and see what the Lord says.

Saul:	We want an answer.
St Peter:	You'll get one.
	(ST PETER exits. The remaining characters stand and glare at each other.)
Solomon:	Oh boy. I wonder what it will be.
Saul:	It'll be a recipe, I bet.
Rebecca:	That's it, a recipe for the Divine Sticky Stuff and how much to put in. We'll be able to make our own. We'll be the greatest stickability types of all time.
All three:	Yea, the answer. You beaut. *(General racket from all three.)*
Ruth:	You've got it all wrong. If only you'd let me explain.
	(All three shout her down. ST PETER enters.)
Rebecca:	Did you get the answer?
St Peter:	I have the answer, yes.
Saul:	Read it. Read it. I want to have more sticky stuff than anyone else.
Solomon:	I want to stick to my job. Is it applied externally or orally?
Rebecca:	I'll even sniff it if I have to.
St Peter:	The answer is—
All three:	Sshhhh!
St Peter:	Thus saith the Lord. Here are the amounts of Divine Sticky Stuff that were instilled into the characters of the people concerned: Solomon—15 grams Saul—15 grams Rebecca—15 grams...
All three:	Yea, it wasn't much, eh?
St Peter:	Ruth—15 grams.
Solomon:	What?
Saul:	It's the exact same amount.
Rebecca:	Gimme that thing here. *(Grabs the paper from ST PETER and reads it.)* That's what it says here. Hey—there's something more on the back. *(Hands it back to ST PETER.)* Here. Read it.
	(The stage lights dim, leaving a single spot on ST PETER or, if there are no stage lights, characters step back and freeze as ST PETER steps forward to read.)
St Peter:	You blame me when things are not as you want. When will you learn to take responsibility for your own actions? I asked you to follow me, to stand by my side and to spread my message to others. I have given you all the ability to carry out your task, but when you fail to use it you make excuses, saying: "This part of me can be for God and this part for myself". But where has this led? It has brought you to your own destruction. You have been made in my image. It is your love I seek, not your complaints and excuses.

You already have the strengths you need. Everyone is the same. None are disadvantaged, save in this—that they do not use what they are given. Now go and try again. I will support you.

(ST PETER bows his head. He is the only character illuminated as the curtains close. If no special lighting is available, characters may exit quietly at the end of the speech, with ST PETER bringing up the rear.)

THE DIVINE STICKY STUFF PATTER

(Ruth): Hel-lo everybody my name is Ruth   Everything I tell you is the

honest truth   I stayed with Naomi my   dear old ma

even though our journey took us   off so far   I   stuck to my friends right

from the start   And   won myself a husband with a   kind warm heart

oh yeah. (Reb.): I   hope the others aren't   coming too oh   dear looky there I

spoke too soon (Saul): And   who are you   tell us your name   (Shad.): I'm

Shadrach the Jew of   furnace fame they   tried to get me to bow

to their rules but   me and my friends   we   aint no fools   we

BIBLE READINGS

Hebrews 12:1-2
1 Corinthians 15:58
1 Peter 5:9
Hebrews 6:19

For background on the characters:
1 Samuel 15:10-29
1 Samuel 18:6-16
1 Kings 11:1-3
Ruth 1:1-17
Daniel 3:8-19
Acts 9:36-41

QUESTIONS FOR DISCUSSION

1. Why is it important for Christians to stick to the task God has allotted to us?

2. When is it most difficult to stick to the task we have been given?

3. The ability to persist with a difficult task provides an excellent witness. How?

4. What problems can make it difficult to stick to our God-allotted tasks? What can help us?

5. In what ways does Ruth provide an effective contrast to Saul and Solomon?

6. In what ways did Jesus show stickability? Why should we be grateful that he did?

THE PAYBACK STORE

CHARACTERS

Customer 1
Sales Assistant
Granny
Footballer
Teenager
Gary

SCENE: *The curtain is closed. The jingle is played from backstage or, if there is no curtain, a live group may sing it as counter is set up for the shop scene.*

JINGLE: If you want to get them back and you don't know how to;
If you are about to crack we can show you how to.
Come down to the Payback Store ... we know we can help you.
If you want to get 'em back, here's all you have to do:

You've got to get 'em back, get 'em back, get 'em back good.
You've got to get 'em back, get 'em back, get 'em back good.
Kick 'em, bash 'em, shoot 'em to bits;
Send 'em poison choccies to give 'em zits.
We've got these and many more
Down at your local Payback Store.
Ahoooooo.

(Curtain opens. CUSTOMER 1 enters. SALES ASSISTANT is behind counter or table.)

Customer 1: Morning, is this the Payback Store?

Sales Assistant: It certainly is, sir. We specialise in all forms of payback, back-biting and revenge supplies, the stuff that everyone needs when the situation really gets out of hand and you just can't stand it any more and you can't let that rotten crud get away with chatting up your girlfriend and he sends you threatening letters in the mail and insults you in front of all your mates, for whom no torture is bad enough. *(Getting carried away now.)* And you want to rip his arms off with our axes and chains. *(Grabs customer and starts to beat his head against the table.)* And guns and racks and clubs. And all at discount prices.

Customer 1: Well, I'd like something special.

Sales Assistant: Of course, sir. We have a wide range of special things. After all, we are the biggest dealer in this area, purveyors by imperial edict to Idi Amin. Our family has been in this business a long time. Anything particular in mind? *(Opens catalogue.)*

Customer 1: No.

Sales Assistant: Well, let's have a look at the range and see. How about something with a continental flavour? We have the guillotine used by the French peasants to get back at the aristocracy for oppressing them. Something in the good old-fashioned English line? Perhaps the axes and dungeons used by Henry the Eighth to get back at his wives? Actually, if you're interested in accommodation I could call in our real estate man ... Oh blow! He's out inspecting the Tower of London and the Black Hole of Calcutta. We also have racks and chains ...

Customer 1: Er, have you anything a little more modern?

Sales Assistant: Space age design? Certainly, including the old cruelty with the advantages of modern techniques ... Laser beams, flick knives, recoilless semi-automatic rifles, ICB missiles for those stubborn types. Out the back we also have our tank yard and mercenary training centre if you want a really extensive revenge job.

Customer 1: No, I think something smaller. It is a domestic situation. I need something small and annoying that cuts deeply but leaves no trace.

Sales Assistant: Well sir, in cases like this we usually recommend a combination of telephone gossip *(begins to mix with bottles and potions)*, some back-biting and subtle insult, social ostracism and finally a pinch of nagging always aimed at weak spots.

Customer 1: Sounds fine to me. Er, your ad said something about a bonus today.

Sales Assistant: Ah, but of course, sir, with every purchase today we supply free a bottle of conscience antidote, for relief of those little niggling thoughts that come up now and then about this sort of thing being wrong.

Customer 1: Rubbish!

Sales Assistant: Of course, sir. Well, good day.

Customer 1: Good day. Oh, is it a little quiet today or something?

Sales Assistant: Oh no, business usually hots up after breakfast time. Little fights and arguments from last night and so on, you know. Should be starting up about now.

(Crowd clamours in and charges for counter.)

Quiet, quiet. Now, who was first?

(All clamour.)

Sales Assistant: How about this dear little old lady first? Now, dear, what would you like?

Granny: Well, I'm a bit upset with little Johnny, the boy who mows my grass for me. You see, it took me three months to get my garden in order and then yesterday he mowed right over my geraniums. After all the cold drinks I poured for him! I said, "You're a naughty little lad, Johnny", and do you know what he did? He laughed at me.

Sales Assistant: That's terrible. What would you like to hire?

Granny: Well, I want a bren gun with .303 lead point bullets so I can shoot the sunshine out of the little brat and throw him down the drain. And I'd also like some epsom salts to put in his next cold drink too.

Sales Assistant: Certainly.

Granny: And if it doesn't work, I'll come back and burn your shop out.

Sales Assistant: Certainly, granny.

Granny: Dear little old granny.

Sales Assistant: Dear little old granny.

Granny: That's better. Watch it, buddy. Granny's on the streets.

(Exit GRANNY.)

Sales Assistant: Now, who's next? Yes sir, what can I do for you?

(FOOTBALLER has till this time been vaguely wandering round.)

Footballer: I got my picture in Football Mauler's Weekly. *(Use this name or insert the name of a popular football magazine in your area.)*

Sales Assistant: Now, what do you want?

Footballer: Prop, front row forward.

Sales Assistant: You're a football player, aren't you?

Footballer: No, I'm a football player.

Sales Assistant: Well, you just think about it for a while.

(FOOTBALLER wanders off.)

Now, madam, how about you?

Teenager: I had this terrible argument with mum and dad last night and I really don't think they were reasonable. Oh, you know how they can be. They make me so mad.

Sales Assistant: And just what did they do?

Teenager: Oh, it was family fellowship last night where we all talk and share things, but I wanted to go out to Fifi's Strip Club with Derrick my drunken slobbering punk boyfriend. *(Weeps.)* And they wouldn't let me. Oh, they're so cruel and unreasonable, and now I want to get back at them because Derrick went there by himself and picked up a stripper and now I've lost him and it's all their fault.

Sales Assistant: I see. Well, the best way to handle parents is with the modern methods. Temper tantrums usually get a good response, and playing on people's emotions too. So I'll give you a bottle of lies, some sympathy-seeking instructions, some non-co-operation and some slander should do the trick. There we are.

Teenager: Oh, thank you. Bye bye.

(Exit TEENAGER.)

Sales Assistant: What a little sweety. Now sir, have you considered what you want yet?

Footballer: *(Grabbing Sales Assistant.)* Is your name Henry?

Sales Assistant: No.

Footballer: I didn't think so.

Sales Assistant: What were you wanting, sir?

Footballer: It's that rotten one-eyed referee last Friday night at Lang Park. I want to get him back. Last Friday night in the game this other guy called me a ...

Sales Assistant: Yes yes, we get the picture.

Footballer: So I got him and headlocked him and rammed his head into the ground and kicked him in the kidneys and punched his head in and threw him into the goal posts. And the ref sent me off ... for nuffing! Now I want to get the ref too.

Sales Assistant: Well, you look like a practical man.

Footballer: I'm not practically a man. I'm really a man. Prop, front row, loose head ...

Sales Assistant: Yes yes, we know all that. Well, here's our latest book on how to pull people's arms and legs off. It's for the physically inclined.

Footballer: But I can't read.

Sales Assistant: Here, try this one. It's got pictures.

Footballer: Oh goody. I'll do this one to him, and that one. Hey, look here! They pulled his legs off and put them where his arms are s'posed to be.

Sales Assistant: You've got the book upside down.

Footballer: Oh yeah. Hee hee.

(Exit FOOTBALLER.)

Sales Assistant: Well, sir, looks like you're the last.

Customer 1: Yes. I wonder if you could help me? I've been a bit upset about this other chap at work. He's always insulting me about my religion, my clothes—well anything. Seems to go out of his way to annoy me, does anything that he knows I don't like. I'm sure he's been stealing money from my desk too. I've tried all the normal reactions—counter insults, gossip, slander—but nothing seems to work. He just gets worse.

Sales Assistant: Ah, he sounds like a real cretin. I hate types like this. Let's do it right. We can send in the mercenaries with long-range bazookas and rifles and blast the whole building to smithereens. A few other people could get hurt in the process, but that's normal enough in the revenge process, so who cares?

Customer 1: Er, that seems a bit wide-ranging. Something more selective?

Sales Assistant: Well, we could be subtle and direct a flame-thrower into his office. How about machine gunning him to death?

Customer 1: No.

Sales Assistant: Maybe just as well. Most of our machine and burp guns are out in Afghanistan where the Afghans and Russians are getting back at one another... Axes, knives or clubs?

Customer 1: No.

Sales Assistant: Well, that's about the range.

Customer 1: What's in the box packed away behind there?

Sales Assistant: Where? Oh that. I don't really know. Actually I haven't hired that out for some time. I can't even think... oh, wait on, that might be the forgiveness box.

Customer 1: What's that?

Sales Assistant: Oh, I don't know. Some antiquated idea about not paying them back with something bad but going on loving them anyway or some such. Look, what you want is ...

Customer 1: Take it down. It looks interesting.

Sales Assistant: But it's all rubbish.

Customer 1: No. I want to look.

Sales Assistant: Oh, alright. But we've got a fresh batch of bazookas coming in on Wednesday. *(Takes down box and dusts it down. Looks inside.)*

Customer 1: It's all warm and fuzzy. *(Puts hand in.)* Ow! Got a bit of a bite to it though.

Sales Assistant: Yes, strong little fellow isn't he? Stronger than he looks.

Customer 1: I'll take it.

Sales Assistant: Well, it doesn't cost any money, but...

Customer 1: Yes?

Sales Assistant: Well, all our other gear is long-range and can even be sent anonymously. This has to be delivered personally, so you'll have to get close to the person. Look, we could change it for a machete...

Customer 1: No no, I'll give it a try.

(Exit CUSTOMER 1.)

Sales Assistant: *(Calls after him.)* Let me know how it goes! *(Aside—to audience.)* But I won't hold my breath waiting. He needs something like a bayonet. The forgiveness box didn't even come with an instruction manual. Just an old Bible.

(Lights black out for passing of night. Jingle is sung again. Or SHOP ASSISTANT may signify time passing by putting up a "closed" sign, exiting, then returning a few seconds later and removing the sign. TEENAGER enters.)

Sales Assistant: Well, how did it go?

Teenager: Here, take your rotten gear.

Sales Assistant: But didn't it work?

Teenager: I tried all your useless stuff and it never had one effect. Mum and Dad never batted an eyelid. They just gave me a hug and said it was a stage I was going through. Lies didn't work—just gave me a bad name. Non-co-operation made me feel terrible. I wish I'd never come here. I hate you. *(Dissolves into tears.)*

(GRANNY enters.)

Granny: Well, here's your bren gun.

Sales Assistant: Granny, nice to see you.

Granny: Nice to see you too, girlie. I just came to say...

Sales Assistant: Thank you?

Granny: No. To say you can shove it up your nose! It never worked. I aimed your bren gun at Johnny and the recoil blew me through the plate glass doors on the front verandah. And the flames burned off me moustache and Johnny ran away. Now there's no one to mow my grass. It's eight feet high. The vegie patch is so weedy I had to get the air force to napalm it. Do you know how much that costs? How am I gonna pay for that on the pension?

(FOOTBALLER enters.)

Footballer: Hey you! Remember me?

Sales Assistant: Ah sir. Now surely you...

Footballer: Wipe that smile off your face, buddy. I am gonna total you!

Sales Assistant: But...

Footballer: I'm gonna shove this book down your throat. I did what it told me to and now I'm in court for assault and battery with six million in damages to pay. I ought to...

Granny: *(Hands him the gun.)* Be my guest.

Footballer: I'll wrap it round her skull.

(CUSTOMER 1 walks in, smiling, with GARY.)

Granny: What are you smiling about, buster?

Customer 1: I'd like to introduce you all to Gary. He's the guy I told you about. I forgave him and now we're the best of friends. We play cricket on the same team.

Sales Assistant: Huh? But didn't...

Customer 1: It's great stuff, that forgiveness. It took a while to work, but I really recommend it. As a matter of fact, I'd like to buy that whole batch. It might not always work as well as this, but it's better than trying to wipe people out.

Gary: *(Looking round at angry faces.)* Er, have we interrupted something?

Footballer: No no. I'm just about to get back at this idiot here.

Teenager: I'll scratch her eyes out.

Granny: I'll fricasee her. Look, we've got all this stuff here to use.

Footballer: I'll wrap everything round her skull.

                     (Pause.)

Sales Assistant: Wait, wait! This shop is closed for renovation. From now on we only stock forgiveness. It's good stuff. Here, have some free samples. I recommend you all to take one each...

                     (Curtain closes as she raves on about forgiveness, and customers gather round to get free samples.)

THE PAYBACK STORE JINGLE

BIBLE READINGS

Matthew 6:12-15
Romans 3:5-8
Luke 11:4
Luke 15:11-32
Mark 11:25

QUESTIONS FOR DISCUSSION

1. How can the Christian principle of forgiveness avoid further complications?

2. Why does Jesus say to forgive "seventy times seven"?

3. Does forgiveness mean there is no such thing as justice?

4. What bearing does our forgiveness of others have on God's forgiveness of us?

5. How can we show we have forgiven someone who has done wrong to us?

6. If God forgives us, why try to be good?

7. How can forgiveness be a Christian witness?

THE SOCIETY FOR MUTUAL SELF FLAGELLATION

CHARACTERS

Chairman
Secretary
Member 1
Member 2
Member 3
Member 4

SCENE: *Lights come up on meeting. Chairperson seated out front, members in rows of chairs with note pads, etc. Each has a whip. Alternatively, characters may enter bringing own chairs and generally chatting as they set up.*

CHAIRMAN: The monthly meeting of the Society for Mutual Self Flagellation will now come to order. Members, quiet please.

(Chatter hushes.)

The salute, please. What do we want?

ALL: Punishment!

CHAIRMAN: When do we want it?

ALL: Now!!

CHAIRMAN: What are we?

ALL: Worms!!!

(They all whip each other vigorously. Screams and yells, etc.)

MEMBER 1: I am a worm!

MEMBER 2: I am a worm!

MEMBER 3: I am a worm!

ALL: *(Singing.)* Worm!

CHAIRMAN: Subdue yourselves, oh fellowship of filth.

(More whipping.)

Subdue your fleshly desires.

(More vigorous whipping still.)

Harder! Louder!

(Louder yells, etc.)

Right, enough. Order, please.

(Clamour ceases and members seat themselves again.)

Secretary, report the minutes of last month's meeting.

SECRETARY: Last month's meeting was held here. It was a most enjoyable social occasion and we all had a great time.

CHAIRMAN: What?! Enjoyable time? Subdue him, quickly!!

(Members all whip secretary into apologetic submission.)

CHAIRMAN: Now, read again, please, without that licentious levity.

SECRETARY: We all had an awful time, but through self punishment we subdued our dastardly bodies and achieved greater purity of spirit.

CHAIRMAN: That's better. Remember, what are we?

ALL: *(Beginning singing again and beating each other.)* Worms!

CHAIRMAN: Right, that's enough. Save the rest for the bed of nails supper after the meeting. Have we any apologies, oh brotherhood of bilge?

MEMBER 1: I apologise for myself. I'm sorry. I'm a rotten sinner, a filthy grovelling mortal. I think bad thoughts. I have not used my talents to their full potential. I am a worm...

ALL: *(On cue all others sing their parts)* Worm!

CHAIRMAN: Congratulations, oh sister of stench. You are making real progress. You are gaining a truly humble self image.

MEMBER 2: I'm humbler than her! She might be a sinner, but I'm a dreadful sinner. I'm positively wicked. And I know it.

MEMBER 3: Oh yeah? That's nothing. I dislike myself. Ooh, I make myself so mad.

MEMBER 1: Yeah, well I abhor myself. I look in the mirror every morning and feel sick.

MEMBER 2: Well, I can't stand to be in the same room with myself!

MEMBER 3: But you **are** in the same room as yourself.

MEMBER 2: Oh yes. So I am. Urrgh! *(Hits himself.)* Get away from me!

MEMBER 3: Well, I'm following the biblical injunction to cut your hand off and throw it away if it causes you to sin. But my whole body causes me to sin, so I'm trying to figure out how to cut my whole body off.

MEMBER 1: Start with your head, garlic features. Then you'll still be able to think.

MEMBER 3: Oh yeah? What would you know, you grovelling, snivelling worm?

MEMBER 1: Thank you. I didn't realise you thought so highly of me.

(They shake hands amiably.)

CHAIRMAN: All right, all right! You're all doing well and you're all great.

(General clamour.)

All right, you're all awful and you're all doing terribly.

(General agreement. Resume seats.)

Now, suggestions for the Christmas breakup activity for this year range widely. Hiking to Canterbury Cathedral on our knees while beating ourselves with ironbark branches.

(General clamour to the effect that this is not bad enough.)

A trip to the Snowy Mountains to stand in ice water neck deep and pray for forgiveness.

(General clamour as above.)

Free passes for all members to the next church synod.

(Clamour to the effect that this is bad enough.)

Right. It's settled then. Now, you citizens of cesspools—the credal statement.

(All stand. The following is effective if chanted in "singsong school playground" style.)

What are we?

ALL: We are sinners.

CHAIRMAN: What type of sinners?

ALL: Filthy sinners, awful sinners, dreadful sinners, smelly sinners...

CHAIRMAN: That's enough.

ALL: We are sorry.

CHAIRMAN: What made us sinners?

ALL: We were proud.

CHAIRMAN: What made us proud?

ALL: We thought we mattered. *(Chant style ends with this line.)*

CHAIRMAN: And do we matter?

ALL: Nooo!!

CHAIRMAN: Are we significant?

ALL: Nooo!!

CHAIRMAN: What are we?

ALL: Sinners.

CHAIRMAN: Do we like ourselves?

ALL: Nooo!!

MEMBER 4: I do.

CHAIRMAN: What?!

(General gasp.)

MEMBER 1: Radical.

MEMBER 2: Communist.

MEMBER 3: Bedwetter.

MEMBER 1: Don't you know self love leads to pride?

MEMBER 2: It makes you think you are better than everyone else.

MEMBER 3: It's the original sin. You try to make yourself God.

MEMBER 4: No I don't. I just think I'm all right.

MEMBER 1: You think you're the best. Sinner!

MEMBER 4: No. But I think I'm just as good.

MEMBER 2: Good? Good is for disgusting world-centred self-centred sinners. They think they are good at things or just good. You are a worm.

MEMBER 4: Okay. I make mistakes. But I'm not all that useless. Anyway, I've got a good friend, and he thinks I'm okay.

MEMBER 3: A friend? A friend? You've got a friend? Who?

MEMBER 4: God.

CHAIRMAN: God? God! God is your friend? How dare you take the Lord's name in vain?

MEMBER 1: Do you think the Lord cares about you? In all the universe, its immensity and diversity, do you think God is going to take any notice of you, you worm?

MEMBER 4: Well, it says in the Bible he even knows how many hairs are on my head.

MEMBER 2: Well there'll be a few less if you blaspheme any more.

MEMBER 3: Don't you understand that God is the pivot point of reality, the ground of being?

MEMBER 1: The maintenance and sustenance of the entire universe depends on him. It is he who lights the sun...

MEMBER 2: Who sets the stars on their courses...

MEMBER 3: Who directs the winds.

MEMBER 1: You think God is going to take any notice of you, you speck of dust?

MEMBER 2: One of the four billion others on this planet.

MEMBER 3: Yeah!

CHAIRMAN: Only those who punish and cleanse themselves are worthy of God's attention.

MEMBER 4: But I've spoken to him personally.

CHAIRMAN: What!?

MEMBER 4: In prayer.

MEMBER 1: Oh, prayer eh? You think God listens to you? And what punishment do you inflict upon yourself while praying?

MEMBER 4: None.

MEMBER 2: Blasphemer.

MEMBER 4: None is necessary.

CHAIRMAN: Oh, he prays, does he? Well, we'll show you how to pray. Come on, boys.

(General grovelling session on the floor. Cries of "sorry" etc.)

There. Can your prayers do any better than that?

MEMBER 4: Well, I also thank the Lord for things he's given me. When I do wrong things, I repent and tell the Lord I'm truly sorry, and he forgives me.

MEMBER 3: Forgives? God forgives you?

MEMBER 4: That's what I was trying to tell you. Jesus loves us.

CHAIRMAN: Us? But we're worms. Unworthy creatures. He must have terrible taste in friendships.

MEMBER 4: He loves us and died for us to forgive our sins.

MEMBER 1: No more whipping?

MEMBER 4: Why? The price is paid. God loves us and wants us to be his friends.

MEMBER 2: But there must be something we can flagellate ourselves about. Shouldn't we hate ourselves just a little bit?

MEMBER 4: No, our sins are all forgiven. We are free from all this self punishment and can follow the special tasks that God has prepared for us to do.

MEMBER 3: You mean all our whipping has been in vain? We can't make ourselves good by putting ourselves down?

MEMBER 4: That's about the size of it. If God died for us and has given us tasks to do, he must love us. And if he loves us, then I guess we should love ourselves also. That's good enough for me.

CHAIRMAN: I'm sorry. We'll have to think about this one. Time out, please.

(Offstage a whistle is blown. All members go into a football huddle.)

We'll have to toss this idea about a bit.

(They execute a football lineout and run across stage passing an imaginary ball and score a try with it. Then all agree generally with the idea proposed.)

Right. It's agreed. We accept. The first inaugural meeting of the Society of Mutual Self Respect and Christian Love will come to order.

(Lights fade as members resume seats, toss away whips. General chatter over new meeting procedure.)

BIBLE READINGS

Matthew 10:29-31
Matthew 22:34-40
Genesis 1:26-28
Ephesians 2:4-9
Matthew 18:10-11.

QUESTIONS FOR DISCUSSION

1. What wrong ideas about themselves and God were exhibited by the members of the Mutual Self Flagellation Society?

2. What does the command to "love your neighbour as you love yourself" suggest about the way we should regard ourselves?

3. Are the things that make us important to God different from the things that make us important to other people?

4. What is false humility? Is it as dangerous as conceit?

5. Why are we valuable to God?

© 1990 THE JOINT BOARD OF CHRISTIAN EDUCATION
The Divine Sticky Stuff: 20 short plays for churches
by Chris Chapman, Susan Chapman, Peter Gregory and Heather Allison

THE GIFTS OF THE SPIRIT

CHARACTERS

Person 1
Person 2
Person 3

SCENE:	*PERSON 1 and PERSON 2 walk onto stage arguing.*
PERSON 1:	I have more gifts of the Spirit than you do.
PERSON 2:	You do not. I have more than you.
PERSON 1:	But mine are better.
PERSON 2:	Are not.
PERSON 1:	Well, what can you do?
PERSON 2:	I can speak in tongues.
PERSON 1:	Of men?
PERSON 2:	And of angels.
PERSON 1:	So what? I can interpret.
PERSON 2:	Big deal. If I didn't speak, you wouldn't have anything to interpret.
PERSON 1:	Well, if I didn't interpret, there'd be no point in your speaking.
PERSON 2:	Big deal. I can prophesy.
PERSON 1:	Oh yeah? So prophesy unto us.
PERSON 2:	Someone is going to hit you.
PERSON 1:	Where??
	(Looks around and PERSON 2 hits him.)
PERSON 2:	See. Told you.
PERSON 1:	Oh yeah, well I can preach.
PERSON 1:	Well, don't preach to me. I have the gift of healing.
PERSON 2:	Well, I have the gift of seeing people's gifts, and you haven't got any of the gifts you say you have.
PERSON 1:	You also have the gift of talking a lot of rubbish.
PERSON 2:	Oh yeah? You think you know everything about the gifts of the Spirit.
PERSON 1:	Well, the way you carry on, anyone would think...
	(They improvise a loud argument.)
PERSON 3:	*(Walking on and hearing the row.)* Hey, what's the problem?

THE GIFTS OF THE SPIRIT

PERSON 1:   He says he's got more gifts than me.

PERSON 2:   I do not. But I have.

PERSON 1:   Well, mine are top quality gifts. They're better.

PERSON 3:   What's all this about being better?

PERSON 2:   Mine are better than his.

PERSON 1:   Are not.

PERSON 3:   But haven't you read 1 Corinthians 12:11?

PERSONS 1 & 2: No.

PERSON 3:   It says, "It is the one and the same Spirit who does all this; as he wishes, he gives a different gift to each person". So you see, we are all equal. No one is any higher than anyone else and no one has cause to boast.

PERSON 2:   That makes sense to me.

PERSON 1:   Me too.

PERSON 2:   Friends?

PERSON 1:   Brothers.

(They shake hands, etc.)

PERSON 2:   After all, we Christians who are filled with the Spirit have to stick together.

PERSON 1:   Exactly.

PERSON 3:   That's better. Well, see you later.

PERSONS 1 & 2: 'Bye.

PERSON 1:   Great guy. He really smooths a bad situation down.

PERSON 2:   Yeah. He's got a real gift.

(They both suddenly realise what has been said and what has happened, and look first at one another and then after the retreating figure. Lights fade, or characters freeze.)

BIBLE READINGS

1 Corinthians 12
1 Corinthians 13
Galatians 5:21

QUESTIONS FOR DISCUSSION

1. What are the "gifts of the Spirit"? Is one gift more important than another?

2. Why are the gifts of the Spirit given?

3. How can the various gifts of the Spirit bring the church closer together?

4. Why do people sometimes argue about the gifts of the Spirit?

5. Should persons not be classified as Christians until they display a certain gift?

6. What gifts do you see present among the members of this group?

© 1990 THE JOINT BOARD OF CHRISTIAN EDUCATION
The Divine Sticky Stuff: 20 short plays for churches
by Chris Chapman, Susan Chapman, Peter Gregory and Heather Allison

THE LONE CHRISTIAN

CHARACTERS

Barmaid
Bartender
Messenger
Cowboys
Bad guy 1
Bad guy 2
Bad guy 3
Lone Christian
Cavalry 1
Cavalry 2
Cavalry 3
Voice over
Guitarist

SCENE: *The curtains open on typical saloon bar scene—the bar (a couple of tables) runs left to right up stage. A couple of cowboys are drinking at a small table (or at the bar). BARTENDER behind and BARMAID in front of the bar, talking. All characters talk with exaggerated and slow accents, as in cowboy movies.*

Barmaid: Is quiet tonight, here in the Silver Dollar Coffee Shop.

Bartender: Yup, nothing to do but shine these here coffee cups.

Barmaid: Yup.

Bartender: Mah wrist is gettin' mighty sore. How is the cinnamon toast supply goin'?

Barmaid: Runnin' mighty low.

Bartender: Ah got some more comin' in on the next stage from Dodge City.

Barmaid: Sure is quiet without the Christian cavalry in here. They're normally all in town talkin' and drinkin' coffee, straight.

Bartender: Yup, sure is quiet in this here town.

Barmaid: Coffee?

Bartender: Nup. Never drink coffee during the day. It keeps me awake.

Barmaid: How come you always are a-talkin' so slow?

Bartender: 'Cause ah plumb forgot mah lines and ah gotta make it up as ah go.

Messenger: *(Runs in, yelling.)* Halp! Halp! Get the sheriff. Quick, call out the Christian cavalry.

Bartender: Why? What's up?

Barmaid: Why? What's up?

Cowboys:	Belch.
Messenger:	It's the Temptation Gang. They've hit town.
Bartender:	Gasp.
Barmaid:	Scream.
Cowboys:	Belch.
Messenger:	They're gunna shoot up all the good guys, an' they're gunna burn the church down, an' they're gunna take over this town for the big boss.
All:	Aghhh!
Messenger:	Ahm a-goin' ta get the Christian cavalry.

(Exit MESSENGER and COWBOYS. As they leave, BAD GUYS enter from opposite side. BARMAID goes to run, but they grab her.)

Bad Guy 1:	Now hold it, honey. Just where you runnin' to?
Bad Guy 2:	We's got a powerful lot of trail dust to wash down.
Bad Guy 3:	So how's about you gettin' us a shot of red eye and then singin' us a long sad song?
Bartender:	You handle her roughly and you'll see what happens. *(The BAD GUYS fling her across stage and she yells as she hits the BARTENDER.)* See. That's what happens. *(Evil laughter from BAD GUYS.)*
Bad Guy 1:	And youse folks better watch out too, 'cause we is the Temptation Gang. Ah'm Rusty Morals.
Bad Guy 2:	And ah'm the Apathy Kid.
Bad Guy 3:	And ah'm Miscellaneous Naughtiness.
All:	And we're the Temptation Gang.

(BARMAID brings drinks to them.)

Bad Guy 1:	Well, what is we gunna do in this town? How can we mess up all the Christians round here?
Bad Guy 2:	Well, ah think the first thing we do is attack the Christian cavalry fort.
Bad Guy 3:	Right, the church. We attack it and burn it down.
Bad Guy 1:	While the Christian cavalry are out on patrol.
Bad Guy 2:	But what can we do to **them**?
Bad Guy 3:	We'll attack them one by one. They're too hard to hit when they're sticking together. You can never surround 'em.
Bad Guy 1:	Yep. I reckon we do the church fort first and then hit 'em singly.
Bad Guy 2:	We'll head 'em off at the pass.
Bad Guy 3:	Ah got a itchy trigger finger.
Bad Guy 1:	Ah is just dyin' to shoot holes in their li'l ole John 3:16.

Bad Guy 2:	And their 23rd Psalm.
Bad Guy 3:	In that case we'll head 'em off at the passage.
Bad Guy 1:	We'll really take over this town, an' the big boss will be real pleased with us.
	(Evil laughter from BAD GUYS.)
Bad Guy 2:	And we is gunna start with youse. *(He turns to the BARTENDER and BARMAID.)*
Barmaid:	No, no, please. I don't wanna be bad, do I boss?
Bartender:	Why no. She's always been good ... ah think.
Barmaid:	Mercy, good sirs.
Bad Guy 1:	Don't call me good, girlie.
Bad Guy 2:	Yeah, we is gunna put youse up against the wall and shoot temptations at you.
Bad Guy 3:	Yeah, from our Cult 45's. Just think... *(Looking at his gun.)* ... somewhere in there, there's a temptation with your name on it.
	(The BAD GUYS swagger over, take the old BARTENDER and roughly push him across to the wall.)
Bartender:	No, no, we always been good, kindly people.
Barmaid:	Why, you great lummoxes, manhandling an old fella like that. You'll pay for that. *(The BAD GUYS give her several coins or dollar notes.)* Ooooo, want another go? *(The BAD GUYS take her over to the wall next to the BARTENDER.)*
Barmaid:	Oh, where are the Christian cavalry?
Bartender:	Probably out horsin' round.
Barmaid:	Stop it. Don't you know this is a serious situation?
Bartender:	Nope, but if you whistle a few bars I might catch on.
Barmaid:	How can you joke around at a time like this?
Bartender:	Because I sense that help is comin'.
Barmaid:	How can you tell?
Bartender:	My years of experience, my sharp eyes, my power of hearing, and my knowledge of the script. The Christian cavalry is comin' to help us fight the temptations.
	(All freeze, lights lowered. Western range music.)
Voice Off:	But who is this we see when we look out across the prairies near this town in trouble? Who is this hombre who rides alone through the tumbleweed? Creaking saddle leather and jingling stirrups echo eerily as he gallops through the dusty sunset, painting in ochre colours the distant Dakota ranges. It is ... the Lone Christian.

(William Tell Overture echoes as lights up and LONE CHRISTIAN enters.)

Lone Christian: Waal, this sure is a quiet coffee shop.

Bad Guy 1: You better mosey on out, stranger.

Bad Guy 2: Or we'll drill you full of temptations.

Bad Guy 3: Yeah, stranger, ride on pronto. Vamoose. You savvy?

Lone Christian: Oh, the Temptation Gang eh? I'll handle you single-handed, 'cause I am the Lone Christian. *(Overture plays in loudly, but he waves it down.)* No, no. That'll be okay, thanks. We had it before.

Bartender: Wait on, pardner, this ain't in the script. You can't handle this on your own. I mean ... how come we never see you at the Christian fort on Sundays?

Lone Christian: 'Cause I am a lone wolf, pardner. As the Lone Christian... *(He points to sound controller to stop overture again.)* I can rely on my own strength and resolve and continue on my lonesome. I don't need the support of other Christians 'cause I can handle it by myself.

Bad Guy 1: No, no. Let him try.

Bad Guy 2: We'll scalp him.

Bad Guy 3: Yeah, stranger, you ain't worth a plugged nickel round here.

Lone Christian: Come on, you guys. This is a showdown.

Bad Guy 1: Where is we gunna slap leather, hombre? In the corral?

Bad Guys 2 & 3: Okay.

(They line up for the fight. BARMAID screams. They all jump with fright and then dive for the floor.)

All: Don't do that!

Barmaid: Sorry.

(Line up again.)

Bad Guy 1: Slap leather, hombre. *(Draws his gun and yells.)* Earthly power.

Lone Christian: *(Draws gun.)* You cannot serve God and money. Luke 16:13.

Bad Guy 2: *(Draws gun.)* Go out and get drunk.

Lone Christian: It is foolish to get drunk. Proverbs 20:1.

Bad Guy 3: *(Draws gun.)* Lower your moral standards.

Lone Christian: Happy are the pure in heart. Matthew 5:9.

Bad Guy 1: Never go to church.

Lone Christian: Eh?

Bad Guys 2 & 3: *(Waving their guns.)* Never go to church.

Lone Christian: Darn, out of ammo. I knew I shouldn't have used that page to wrap up the rubbish.

Bad Guy 1:   Get him, boys. He's out of ammo.

Bad Guy 2:   Get 'em up, gringo. We're gunna send you on the last roundup.

Bad Guy 3:   Say your prayers, pilgrim.

(LONE CHRISTIAN raises hands.)

Barmaid: This is the end for the Lone Christian and all of us.

Bartender: I knew he couldn't handle the Temptation Gang on his own.

Barmaid: What is we gunna do?

Bartender: We is gunna gasp any moment now.

Barmaid: Why is we gunna gasp?

Bartender: Because the Christian cavalry is about to arrive.

(Sound of trumpet from off stage. CAVALRY enter in group.)

Cavalry 1:   What's going on here?

Bad Guy 1:   Oh no!

Bad Guy 2:   It's the ...

Bad Guy 3:   ... Christian cavalry.

Bartender: Coffee and cinnamon toast for six coming up.

Barmaid: The Temptation Gang is holding us to ransom and we can't fight 'em off.

Cavalry 2:   You guys better ride on.

Cavalry 3:   Or we'll run you out of town on a rail.

Bad Guy 1:   Let's vamoose, boys.

Bad Guy 2:   Yeah, but you guys better watch it.

Bad Guy 3:   'Cause we'll be round and we got lots of ammo.

Cavalry 1:   Yeah? Well, we got more ammo than you.

Cavalry 2:   God's ammo.

Cavalry 3:   And the support of each other.

(The BAD GUYS depart, grumbling.)

Barmaid: Oh, we're so glad to see you.

Lone Christian: Oh well, it was nothing...

(The BARMAID rushes past him to the CAVALRY.)

Cavalry 1:   Now who is this stranger?

Cavalry 2:   We never see you around.

Cavalry 3:   Where you from, pardner?

Lone Christian: Oh, around. But why couldn't I beat them temptations? Up to now I been outwitting them just fine.

Cavalry 1: Well, pardner, sometimes you need the support and help of other Christians.

Cavalry 2: That's right. We all get together and God encourages us all together.

Cavalry 3: And it's more interesting. You learn from others as well as having friends.

Lone Christian: Yeah, maybe. But I nearly had them. If only I'd had that other verse.

Cavalry 1: You mean "Let us not give up the habit of meeting together"? Hebrews 10:25.

Cavalry 2: And "where two or three come together in my name, I am there with them". Matthew 18:20.

Cavalry 3: We did them in our Bible study last week. You'd have been okay if you'd been there. See? You do get help and support in church and youth group.

Lone Christian: Maybe you're right. I mean, I can go by myself just so long, but I'll need help some time.

(They shake hands in agreement.)

Bartender: And with that, they joined hands. These is happy tidings. The coffee and cinnamon toast is on the house.

(Everyone shouts and they all crowd around the bar.)

Barmaid: Oh, it is so good now that the Christian cavalry is in town again.

(They all call for drinks. Lights down.)

BIBLE READINGS

Hebrews 10:25
Matthew 18:20
Matthew 16:18
Romans 16:5

QUESTIONS FOR DISCUSSION

1. What are some problems you have faced when out of contact with other Christians?

2. Why does the Lone Christian have trouble facing the Temptation Gang?

3. What are some advantages of having a group of other Christians with whom to meet?

4. "Church assemblies were okay in New Testament times when Christians were being persecuted. They had to stick together. We don't need it now." What do you think?

5. "When Jesus said, 'Where two or three come together in my name, I am there with them', he never meant it to become like an institutionalised church." Respond.

6. What is "the church"?

7. What active roles can young people play in the church?

8. Teenagers and young adults will, in a decade or so, be the leading adult members of the church community. How does this make you feel? How can young people prepare themselves for this role?

9. How can we **tastefully** invite non-Christian friends to church or fellowship?

CHANGE

CHARACTERS

Voice off
Newsreader
Announcer
Jimmy (Not Olsen)
Housewife
Professor
Interjector
Christian

NOTE: *This is a series of mini scripts which was presented as a single segment like a drama collage. They are also effective if presented singly, or in various combinations.*

— Play 1 —

Voice off: Change. Tonight we talk about change. Change. Six letters. C-H-A- N-G-E. People can change. Change people change. John and Jill can change. See Jill change. Good heavens. Don't look. Sorry, Jill.

(NEWSREADER walks out to desk in front of curtain and sits down.)

Newsreader: Good evening. Tonight on "World in One Hour" we consider the ways in which psychologists account for the often radical character changes we see in everyday people, and look at the nature and extent of these changes in personality. Excuse me.

(NEWSREADER takes a drink from glass of water on desk. Burps. Goes into convulsions and goes through a Jekyll and Hyde change, staggering off as a gibbering, hand-wringing, deformed wretch.)

— Play 2 —

Voice off: And now... *(Wild party noises, women screaming, bottles and booze. 5 seconds.)* But enough of *(Insert name of local fellowship group.)* Now onto change again.

Announcer: *(Offstage.)* Hello, ladies and gentlemen. Today we present a few great before and after tests from the super spread company, Perks. Remember, just a little Perk goes such a long way. Today we test the old Saul of Tarsus sandwich with the new improved **Paul** of Tarsus sandwich spread. Well... *(Sound of helicopter.)* Here we are in the Paul of Tarsus spread helicopter and we're over Damascus now—and yes, I can see the supermarket now, so let's go down and interview the typical housewife the Paul of Tarsus spread courtesy girl has found. Take her down, Jimmy the helicopter pilot.

Jimmy: Okay.

(Chops suddenly stop.)

Announcer:	Aghhhhhh!
Jimmy:	Aghhhhhh!

(Fade out to crash. Curtain opens. ANNOUNCER wanders on.)

Announcer: Oh well, here we are where the Damascus supermarket used to be— and not only that, but we wiped out that rotten courtesy girl. Well, here's our housewife.

Housewife: *(Enters.)* Hello.

Announcer: Well, she's not exactly typical, is she? Better than most, actually. Now, madam, how are we today?

Housewife: Well, I was all right until that great Iriquois helicopter landed on me head. I feel all unbalanced now.

Announcer: Now, madam, we have here two slices of bread. This one is spread with the old Saul of Tarsus spread. Taste it and see.

Housewife: *(Stuffs it in.)* Ooh, it's a bit acidic and gritty. Ooh, got a real bite to it. Makes you all angry and aggro like wanting to grab a few Christians and beat their faces in. *(Grabs announcer and shakes him round a bit.)*

Announcer: Well, now that you've tasted that, try the new improved Paul of Tarsus spread.

Housewife: *(Stuffs it in.)* Oh, that's much nicer. Makes you feel peaceful and loving. That's much nicer, mmm.

Announcer: So there it is. Proof that the new Paul of Tarsus spread is 100% better. It's really ... really ... well, it really is. I must stop that ad-libbing.

Housewife: By the way, are you married?

Announcer: Well, heh heh heh. I'd better go now. *(Sidesteps to exit and runs last few paces off stage.)*

Housewife: No, wait. The money I save from buying cheaper Paul of Tarsus spread I'll put in my glory semi-trailer. *(Runs off after ANNOUNCER.)*

(Close curtains or black out.)

— Play 3 —

(Curtain closed or lights blacked out.)

Voice off: Do you ever get jealous of your neighbour's life? How does she get it so bright, clean and white? When it's hanging out on the line, it's dazzling. Chances are, you need to change to "God Flakes Life Washing Powder".

(FX helicopter chops.)

Well, here we are in the "God Flakes Life Washing Powder" helicopter, cruising along—and yes, I can see the typical supermarket we're about to visit and see who our new courtesy girl has for us to talk to. Are you ready, Jimmy the helicopter pilot? Hey, it's cold up here, isn't it?

(Chops stop suddenly.)

Jimmy:	There, I turned off the fan.
Voice off:	Aghhhhh!
Jimmy:	Aghhhhh!

(Fade into smash. ANNOUNCER enters as lights come up.)

Announcer: Well, here we are amidst the ruins of yet another supermarket, wondering where our courtesy girl is. But here comes our housewife again. Well, dear, how's your life?

Housewife: Oh, not very good I'm afraid.

Announcer: Do you think this powder could get your life clean and bright again?

Housewife: "God Flakes Life Washing Powder?" Oh no, I don't think so. All those dirty marks and stains and greasy patches round the collars...

Announcer: Well, let's see. Just go over there and get into that industrial size giant Smalleys washer usually used for oil tanker boilers and take the "God Flakes Life Washing Powder" with you.

(Exit HOUSEWIFE. FX grinding and washing noises, culminating in huge explosion.)

Housewife: *(Enters.)* Well, John, I'm convinced.

Announcer: Convinced that "God Flakes" can get the dirtiest life clean again?

Housewife: Yep, and also convinced that Smalleys needs to make stronger washing machines. By the way, are you married?

Announcer: Heh heh heh. Well, I'd better be going now. *(Escapes as before.)*

Housewife: Come back. I've got a nice new job as a central pylon on the Sydney Harbour Bridge. *(Or insert the name of another bridge.)*

(Exit HOUSEWIFE.)

— Play 4 —

(PROFESSOR enters.)

Professor: Good evening. I am Professor Emmanuel Filthiness, and physics is my business. Let us look back... *(Looks behind him.)* ... at our backs. No, let us look back. In previous skits it was intimated that changes in Paul from a bigotted, fanatical anti-Christian to a zealous supporter of the church were due to the impact of God. And so I ask the question, why is it so? Why do people change? Now let us look back. *(Looks behind him.)*

No, sorry. Let's front the issue while looking sideways at our backs. No, that's not right either. Let's put our feet down our fronts while looking at our backs sideways. Who's got a sideways backside? What a terrible trouble you must have with your clothes. No, there's something wrong there too. Let's look round. I don't look round—I've been on a diet for the past three weeks ... a vegetarian diet. I only eat vegetarians. Ho ho, a joke.

I mean to say, do you really expect me to believe God changed Paul? Give me any known example in the Bible where God changed someone.

Interjector: What about David?

Professor: Shut up.

Interjector: And Jonah.

Professor: Look, be quiet.

Interjector: And Moses.

(PROFESSOR grabs a gun and shoots INTERJECTOR.)

Professor: See, not one example. The idea is totally preposterous, ludicrous and irrational—and besides, I didn't think of it. But here is something I thought of—my theory of change in people. You see, I believe that when we are born there are hundreds of these tiny little people in our heads, miniature Michelangelos. As we grow older, these little painters begin to paint on a giant screen on the inside of our foreheads. Every now and then, of course, they have to clean the screen off. Do you get headaches? That's when they're scraping the paint off. Burning migraines? They're using blowtorches. Throbbing pains? Their local rock group is having a concert. And if you get grinding, awful, twisting agony ... you've caught your head in a meat mincer.

Now, the essence of change is this. Now and then one of these little painters gets retrenched. There are recessions, strikes, unemployment of the mind—a fairly common problem around here. But, as in all healthy economies, there is a resurgence and more painters are put on. **But** they are **different** painters and they paint different pictures. Therefore you get a whole new set of ideas and attitudes. So let's not have any more preposterous ideas about God intervening in people's lives to change them. Isn't it a fantastic theory I've developed? Does anyone believe it? Good. You're as sane as me—and I know I'm sane because this piece of paper certifies that I am, and it's signed by me.

And while I'm at it, let me recommend to you weekend brain surgery. It's fun. Start up on some of the simpler models like... *(Insert appropriate name here.)* If you operate on his mind, be sure to have a good bath straight afterwards. And for goodness sake, if you do any work on... *(Insert another appropriate name.)* ...take along a big stick to knock down the cobwebs. And to conclude this lecture on change, think about this: People in glass houses shouldn't change without the curtains drawn. No, that's not it. When you think of loose change send it to me...

(PROFESSOR exits, trying to figure out a proverb.)

— Play 5 —

(Mild-mannered looking character [CHRISTIAN] enters cautiously, looking around.)

Christian: Hello there. I go to church. I'm a... *(Looks round.)* Shhh... a Christian. I, um, teach Sunday school and take a youth group. But recently I've become very worried. It's hard for me to say this but... well... I've started feeling... **hallelujah!** *(Gasps, hands over mouth.)* ...good. It's awful. I'm usually very quiet, but now I want to talk louder and louder and **tell everyone I'm a Christian!** *(Gasps.)*

Why, it's unheard of. The other night I read three chapters of the Bible and... well... I enjoyed it. "I'm sorry, Lord", I said. "I know your book isn't meant to be treated like that. I'm sorry I enjoyed something. It **must** be a sin." Then last night at youth club I got a sudden urge to read some Bible verses out. "Defend me, Lord", I prayed, but the urge just got stronger, and in the end I did it... a Bible reading. And they enjoyed it! *(Breaks down into tears.)* And we discussed it. A virtual orgy of Bible discussion. No more silly games and kissy kissy down behind the pile of old hymn books near the pulpit. Forgive me for leading these young ones astray.

Oh, what is to become of me? I've become a Christian who tells people of the love of Jesus. I never used to be. I was always a good old fashioned, nominal Christian. I was just like all the other people in the office. For ten years I made sure no one knew there was anything different about me. But now it's all changed. I get these urges to tell people. It's so embarrassing— but I'm just bursting. Oh no. I feel one coming on now. **I'm a Christian and I'm happy!** Oh dear, such language. I'll have to close my mouth and go away now. I'm sorry.

(CHRISTIAN rushes off, trying to hold mouth closed, but obviously is unable to stop the cheers and yells which are about to burst out.)

— Finish —

BIBLE READINGS

Matthew 9:9-13
Luke 19:1-10
Luke 8:2
2 Corinthians 5:17
Ephesians 4:17-24
Acts 9

QUESTIONS FOR DISCUSSION

1. Think of specific examples of lives that have been changed by Jesus.

2. In what ways has your life been changed? (Avoid long personal testimonies!)

3. When a person accepts Jesus, is the change in their life immediate and total or an ongoing process?

4. "Please be patient; God isn't finished with me yet." What does this say to us as Christians?

5. How may the above saying be used as a cop out by Christians?

6. Look at the examples of Matthew, Mary Magdalene, Paul and Zacchaeus. In what ways were they changed?

7. Some people say that dramatic changes in people's lives can be put down to psychological readjustment or coincidence. How do you respond to that?

© 1990 THE JOINT BOARD OF CHRISTIAN EDUCATION
The Divine Sticky Stuff: 20 short plays for churches
by Chris Chapman, Susan Chapman, Peter Gregory and Heather Allison

THE OPERATION

CHARACTERS

Norma Cleaner
Doctor 1
Doctor 2
Nurse

SCENE: *Operating room. Operating table has object covered by cloth. Two DOCTORS operating, assisted by a NURSE. Easily recognised theme music from T.V. medical program is played as the curtain opens.*

Doctor 1: Difficult case, very difficult.

Doctor 2: Can't understand it at all.

Doctor 1: Yes, nurse, hold the light closer please. That's better.

Doctor 2: Maybe... no, it's no use.

Nurse: Totally beyond my comprehension.

Doctor 1: In all my years of training, I've never seen anything this complex.

Nurse: What do you think, doctor?

Doctor 2: Frankly speaking, I've no idea. No idea at all.

Doctor 1: If only there was some fresh insight on this problem.

Doctor 2: We need a new approach.

Nurse: Or there will be no hope.

Doctor 1: An angel.

Doctor 2: A miracle.

Nurse: A genius.

(NORMA CLEANER ambles on stage with a bucket and mop.)

Norma Cleaner: Hello, what are you doing messing up my floor?

Doctor 1: Who are you?

Norma Cleaner: I'm Norma Cleaner. I'm the cleaner, and my name's Norma.

Doctor 2: Do you suppose she could be the cleaner?

Norma Cleaner: *(She doesn't understand the previous comment.)* And furthermore, I'm responsible for the cleanliness of this room.

Doctor 2: Thank heavens you're a cleaner. We'll need someone to clean up the mess after we've finished. But you'll have to stand over in that corner until all this is over.

Nurse: This is a restricted area and only those of us who are trained people can come in.

(NORMA does not move.)

Doctor 1: No ordinary people.

Doctor 2: Only the selected few.

Nurse: No one else could understand.

Norma Cleaner: Well, what are you doing?

Doctor 1: Quiet. Keep away.

Doctor 2: It's extremely delicate.

Nurse: We understand practically nothing about it.

Norma Cleaner: But...

Doctor 1: Don't touch it!

Doctor 2: We don't know what effects it may have.

Nurse: That's why we keep it locked away here, away from ordinary people.

Norma Cleaner: Well, can I see it?

Doctor 1: Well, I don't know.

Norma Cleaner: Do I need safety goggles or something?

Doctor 1: No, I think it should be all right. But for goodness sake be careful.

Doctor 2: And don't touch anything.

(They rip the sheet off.)

Norma Cleaner: But it's only a Bible.

Nurse: Shhh, quiet. Everyone will find out.

Norma Cleaner: But everyone knows about the Bible.

Doctor 1: Well, they shouldn't. It takes trained people like us to deal with this sort of thing.

Norma Cleaner: Well, what are you doing to it?

Doctor 1: We are dissecting it. Trying vainly to extract some of its secrets from its very bowels.

Doctor 2: Not just any part of the Bible.

Nurse: It's Matthew 22 verse 39.

Norma Cleaner: What? All this for one verse.

Doctor 1: Not just any verse, my good woman. It's cryptic.

Doctor 2: It's hidden.

Nurse: It's meaningless. We just don't understand it.

Norma Cleaner: What does it say?

Doctor: Ahem. "Love your neighbour as yourself."

Norma Cleaner: Well, that's pretty basic.

Doctor 1:   Idiot, fool, dullard!

Doctor 2:   You don't just accept these things at face value.

Nurse: They require years of interpretation, study, contemplation.

Norma Cleaner: But it just says love your neighbour as yourself!

Doctor 1:   But don't you see? It's more complex than that.

Norma Cleaner: Sounds simple enough to me.

Doctor 1:   That's because you **are** simple, you air brain!

Norma Cleaner: What did you call me?

Doctor 1:   An air brain.

Norma Cleaner: That's what I thought you called me.

Doctor 2:   You think it's simple. Well, explain this word "love".

Norma Cleaner: Well, it means you like someone, a lot.

Nurse: But how much? It may be an anagram, a simile, a metaphor.

Doctor 1:   What sort of love? Platonic love which passes purely between two intellects?

Doctor 2:   Or physical love between two people, man and woman?

Norma Cleaner: Oooh.

Nurse: Or the comradeship of doomed men on the battlefield?

All three: Well?

Norma Cleaner: Well, I think it means you like people.

Doctor 1:   **Like people?** Do you bring our Lord's complicated words so low? Any ordinary person could understand that. We speak of the Christ, the Logos, the meaning of life, the pivot of the universe...

Doctor 2:   ...unreachable...

Nurse: ...untouchable...

Norma Cleaner: I thought he was quite a nice person myself.

Doctor 1:   Fool. You miss the point.

Doctor 2:   And what about this phrase, you old bag? "Love your neighbour." An imperative command, the active verb passing from the subject to the receiver in the object. Neighbour. Who is it?

Norma Cleaner: Old Mrs Harris next door?

Doctor 1:   No!

Norma Cleaner: The man down the street?

Doctor 2: No!

Norma Cleaner: People overseas?

Nurse: No!

Norma Cleaner: I think he means you like people all over the world no matter who or what they are.

Doctor 1: Idiot.

Doctor 2: You haven't even considered the possibility that this world does not even exist.

Nurse: What about the dream theory? What is real? What is normal? It's completely socially defined and existentially proven. You just accept the primal cause idea at face value like all you ignorant peasants.

Doctor 1: I have a theory.

Doctor 2: Yes?

Nurse: Yes?

Doctor 1: Man is... what man is... what man is... what?

Doctor 2: A question or an accusation?

Nurse: Maybe we'll never know.

Norma Cleaner: You're all silly.

Doctor 1: Why do you say that? Because we question? Because we crave knowledge?

Norma Cleaner: No. Because you're making it all too complicated. Look, it's simple.

(They all gasp.)

Doctor 2: Blasphemer.

Nurse: Communist.

Doctor 1: Bed wetter.

Norma Cleaner: Look, Jesus didn't mean any of that stuff you said. Love your neighbour. It's as simple as that. Just listen to what it says and don't worry about all that complicated rot and...

Doctor 1: Fool! You'll never understand.

Doctor 2: I'll never understand.

Nurse: No one will ever understand.

Doctor 1: It's too complex for our mortal minds to grasp.

Doctor 2: It's hidden from our eyes...

Nurse: Until we see clearly in that great afterlife, not through a glass darkly...

(They go off, mumbling and debating. Spotlight narrows to Norma and the table. She sits down quietly and begins to read aloud.)

Norma Cleaner: Love your neighbour. Seems simple enough to me. Love your neighbour as yourself. It's beautiful.

(Reads on silently as lights fade and curtain closes.)

BIBLE READING

Hebrews 5:11-14

QUESTIONS FOR DISCUSSION

1. The Bible can be studied at very great depth, yet can also be read simply, even by a child. How does our understanding of Bible stories grow and change as we grow older?

2. What are the dangers in making Bible study too deep and complicated? What are the advantages in studying the Scriptures very deeply?

3. What are the dangers in over-simplifying the Bible and its stories and messages?

4. How can we maintain a balance between the simple and the complex?

5. How should Christians study the Bible? Share round the group ways, ideas and methods you could use in your Bible study program.

6. What does Hebrews 5:11-14 say to us about our study of the Bible?

© 1990 THE JOINT BOARD OF CHRISTIAN EDUCATION
The Divine Sticky Stuff: 20 short plays for churches
by Chris Chapman, Susan Chapman, Peter Gregory and Heather Allison

MIX AND MATCH

CHARACTERS

Stevie Loveself
Wendy Wimp
Joanne Christian
Caroline Jetset
Bruce Brisbane
Debbie Nuisance
Boron
Voice off

Note: "Boron" is a computer. Our first production featured BORON played by an actor in a black robe with a hood. The actor squatted so that he was able to move around but appeared very short. You could try an actor squatting with a box on top and arms coming out the sides.

SCENE: *Play opens with a suitable inane jingle similar to those played on T.V. game shows.*

Voice off: ... and tonight, in "Mix and Match", we have three lovely contestants, all playing for a great prize. The winning "Mix and Match" couple will receive an all-expenses-paid night out at a local council meeting to see democracy in action. So come on now, let's meet our three lovely ladies, who are in it to win it!

(Lights come up on stage right to reveal three girls seated in chairs, each with a microphone.)

Contestant Number 1 is Wendy Wimp. Tell us about yourself, Wendy.

Wendy: Hi there. Oh my goodness, it's been such a week, but I've been so excited to be on T.V., you just wouldn't believe it, but here I am, so hello, Aunty May and Uncle Ralph, and Mum—told you I'd make it, Mum, and... *(Looks offstage.)* ...what's that? Tell them what you like, you idiot? Oh yes, nearly forgot. It's that silly man—he's told me I'm nearly out of time...

Voice off: Well, that's Wendy Wimp. She's a Christian, and she likes all sorts of things. Now on to contestant Number 2, Joanne Christian.

Joanne: Hi, I'm Joanne Christian. I'm a Christian and I go to my local church and youth group. I'm 22, and I also enjoy hockey, hiking and playing guitar. I'm a commercial artist, but I'd rather be out in the great outdoors.

Voice off: And contestant Number 3, Caroline Jetset.

Caroline: Hi, I'm Caroline Jetset, and I'm a really active person. I'm 23, and I enjoy parties, hang-gliding with my boyfriend's club, and I'd love to try hot air ballooning. I love to go wind surfing and dune buggying, and we go down

	to the surf most weekends. I like a man who likes going out a lot. Oh... and I'm a Christian, too.
Voice off:	... and there they are, our three lovely ladies for tonight's game. We are certainly in for some action. So now let's meet our hosts for tonight—our own Debbie Nuisance, and our special guest host, Stevie Loveself.
	(Replay the game show theme. Lights up stage right. Enter STEVIE LOVESELF.)
Stevie:	*(Addressing the audience.)* Hi, folks! Are you all happy? *(Encourages the audience to respond.)* I can't hear you... *(Audience responds more loudly.)* Good. Now I'll take this cotton wool out of my ears. Well, let's meet the brave man who's contesting tonight—the lucky man who will win the chance to take one of these lovely ladies on a fabulous all-expenses-paid night out at the local council meeting. Our contestant tonight is a local boy, Bruce Brisbane. *(Or substitute an alliterative name featuring your local community.)* So now, as we welcome him to this corny and commercialised show, let's give him a big hand.
	(BRUCE enters stage left, and sits in a chair. STEVIE approaches.)
	Hi, Bruce.
Bruce:	*(Yelling into STEVIE's ear.)* Hi, Stevie!
Stevie:	I wish you wouldn't do that.
Bruce:	Sorry.
Stevie:	So, tell us a little about yourself.
Bruce:	Well, I'm Bruce Brisbane, and I'm a Christian. I'd like to meet a Christian girl who is really sure where she stands as a Christian, and who demonstrates her faith in a practical way.
Stevie:	Right. So what you are looking for is a girl whose actions perfectly match her faith. Right. Great concept. Well, we've got a great bunch of competitors tonight. But before we start, we've one more very important person to meet. It's our compatibility computer, who rates our contestants' compatibility. Let's meet Boron.
	(Enter DEBBIE and BORON.)
Debbie:	Tonight, Boron rates our contestants as...
Stevie:	Shhh, not yet. Wait until I say the word "score".
	(DEBBIE retreats with BORON.)
	Well, it's down to business for tonight's show. Bruce, you may ask the first question.
Bruce:	You have all stated you are Christians, but what do you do in your spare time that demonstrates your faith?
Wendy:	Well, I really like going to our local youth group, and it's only on occasions that I don't go.

Bruce:	When don't you go?
Wendy:	Well, I don't go on witnessing nights, or when I have to take the devotions, because I don't like the stress. I find it hard to cope. And I like to avoid visiting the old people's home when the youth group goes, 'cause they pressure you into talking to them. And I usually don't go to working bees either. Work's no good when you wear white clothes.
Bruce:	Well, when do you go?
Wendy:	I went last week, when we went ten pin bowling.
Stevie:	Well, contestant Number 2, it's your turn.
Joanne:	Well, I play keyboards in a band. I like Indian cooking and spending some time with my fellowship group—they're a really great bunch of people—well, they're my best friends. We do a lot of things together. We go to all the organised activities in our church and youth group, but we also just spend time together—you know—playing sport, talking, and all that stuff.
Stevie:	Great answer. Now Number 3.
Caroline:	Well, my spare time is taken up with lots of going out and socialising. I go to church and fellowship group, but I didn't last week 'cause Kathy had a great party on, and it's rude to say no when she'd invited me. Mmmm, come to think of it, I didn't go the week before either. Now whose party was that...?
Stevie:	Well, let's see how those answers scored and...
Debbie:	And tonight, Boron rates the compatibility of Bruce Brisbane as...
Stevie:	We haven't finished yet!
Debbie:	What?
Stevie:	It's not time for that yet!
Debbie:	Oh, sorry.
Stevie:	Bright girl, that. And now Bruce, you may ask your second question. And remember—this is your final question, or else this show will run on into boring insanity, just like the ones on T.V.
Bruce:	If I didn't know you and I met you, how would I know you were a Christian without you telling me?
Stevie:	Contestant Number 1.
Wendy:	Oh well, I'm a nice person. I smile a lot, and... um.. I carry a Bible in my purse. And I wear white a lot to symbolise purity.
Stevie:	Contestant Number 2.
Joanne:	Well, I probably would have told you at some point. I like to make it plain just where I stand. I try to live the way Jesus lived, and the way he wants us to. I don't always succeed, but I do try.
Stevie:	And the final contestant...

Caroline: Um... well... I think... yes, I have a 25 carat gold cross around my neck, with an emerald scratch-and-sniff centre, and when you press it, it plays "Nearer my God to thee". If that's not spiritual, I don't know what is.

Stevie: How can you argue with that? I'm sure you'll all score highly.

Debbie: Well, tonight's compatibility rating...

Stevie: Don't you dare!

Debbie: Sorry.

Stevie: Well, the moment of truce, Bruce... Ah, I mean **truth**, Bruth... I mean, this is it! Are you nervous?

Bruce: Yes, a bit.

Stevie: Before you tell us your choice, Bruce, tell us how you were able to choose the right girl.

Bruce: I chose her because her lifestyle matched up with her statement about being a Christian. It's important to me that my girl knows where she stands, and isn't afraid to tell everyone.

Stevie: Okay, Bruce, tell us now—who did you choose as your "Mix and Match"?

Bruce: Contestant number 2.

(All girls smile brightly. WENDY and CAROLINE scowl and sneer when JOANNE gets up.)

Stevie: What a surprise! *(Waits for the girls to settle down.)* Well, Bruce, come and meet your "Mix and Match".

(The couple greet each other and go to kiss, but STEVIE butts in between them.)

... and don't forget, we've got to find out how our compatibility computer rated the contestants. So now it's over to Debbie and Boron... *(Pause.)* Debbie and Boron... Now, Debbie!!!

Debbie: Oh, are we on now? Sorry.

Stevie: Do your stuff!

Debbie: Oh, ummm... I've forgotten my lines now.

Stevie: *(Tearing at his hair.)* Ahhhh boy, will I ever be pleased to get back to reading the weather report, where you work with real professionals.

Boron: Ah, excuse me, earthlings. Am I correct in surmising that you wish me to use my amazing powers of estimation and deduction to determine the compatibility of these two contestants? If that is so, I deduce that they have a compatibility rating of 97.3%, and I think she's a great lady. Bruce, you are a lucky man.

Stevie: Well, that's a great ending for a show which borders on the ridiculous. That's all for tonight. 'Bye kids!

(Fade lights on scene as the program theme plays.)

BIBLE READINGS

James 2:14-26
Luke 10:25-37

QUESTIONS FOR DISCUSSION

1. What does faith mean to each of the three contestants in the play?

2. What might a Christian look for in a partner? How does this differ from what anyone else might seek in a partner?

3. Jesus had a lot to say about hypocrisy. How does this connect with the idea of "faith without works"?

4. Why is "faith without works" not true faith?

5. Discuss the concept of "works without faith". What do you think God would say about this?

THE POWER SOURCE

CHARACTERS

Voice off
Pong
General Mess
Superperson
Amelia Nice

SCENE: *The Floating Pong Chinese Space Restaurant. If possible, this scene should feature a projection screen as a backdrop. (In one production we used a large OHP screen to project simple drawings of the planet, the noodle belt and the spaceship smashing into it. This was fun and the audience loved it.) Remember, these drawings should really look fake. On the screen will be shown a range of drawings (such as the planet scenes mentioned above), an electric stove and some messages. Before PONG enters the planet scenes should change to a drawing of the electric stove. Enter PONG.*

Voice off: And now another episode in the adventures of Superperson, superhero in training. You will remember that, in previous chapters, Superperson has waged a continual struggle against the evil, cunning and socially unacceptable Emperor Pong the merciless and his servant General Mess. However, though they were ignominiously expelled from the scene of their latest crime, we have not heard the last of these two.

Now we follow them to Pong's dastardly hideout, in the back rooms of a down-town Chinese space restaurant, floating in the depths of the star cluster known as the Soy system, deep in the noodle belt. As we join the story, Pong's enormous rice-powered chopstick ship approaches the parking area of the Floating Pong Chinese Space Restaurant. *(Sound effect of a smash.)*

Pong: Always did hate reverse parking. Mess, come here.

Mess: *(Entering, pretending to be a waiter.)* Evening sir, welcome to the Floating Pong Restaurant.

Pong: No, it's me, fool.

Mess: No, sir. The Mee Fool Restaurant is down the road. May I recommend the chef's specialty, marinated budgie beak in pong sauce, cooked under plessure with eleven different herbs and spices...

Pong: Shut up. It's me. Pong the merciless.

Mess: Master! You have returned disguised as yourself. It's brilliant.

Pong: Come with me, idiot, into the dim, back rooms of the restaurant and we will make big plans.

Mess: Yes, master. But first I must serve the customer.

Pong:	Which customer?
Mess:	This one. Wait on, weren't you in here before?
Pong:	This is me, fool.
Mess:	Thought I recognised you. But I told you, the Mee Fool Restaurant is down the road.
Pong:	No, that was me.
Mess:	So you came back. Food no good at Mee Fool Restaurant?
Pong:	Get out the back, fool. *(Pushes him to the other side of the stage.)* Mess, I am on the verge of a great breakthrough.
Mess:	You should take a holiday, master. You've been working too hard.
Pong:	No, a breakthrough, not a breakdown. Mess, have you ever thought?
Mess:	No, master. It hurts.
Pong:	No, fool. Have you ever thought about this universe—what created it, what holds it together?
Mess:	Stick-all glue?
Pong:	What holds the planets in motion, causes the tides to ebb and flow, the stars to shine, the suns to burn? Imagine...
	(MESS sings the first few lines of any song about imagining.)
	Quiet! I can't stand punk rock. Imagine that power that created all this. It must be the ultimate power in reality. Think what it could mean if we could harness that power for our use.
Mess:	Like **the** force, master?
Pong:	Yes, Mess. But infinitely greater, beyond imagination. Greater than solar, nuclear, steam, electricity, all other power sources. If we could divert that power—harness it—we could power the greatest weapons system in the cosmos. Control everything. Be masters of reality.
Mess:	But how, master?
Pong:	Well, we have all we need right here in the electric stove.
Mess:	Master?
Pong:	Well, you know what they say—there ain't nothing you can't fix with a bit of fencing wire. We can wire up the stove elements to the wok. You hold it. That can be the transceiver. Now the current will zap down into the wok and we'll focus it into the elements, which will increase the power by a factor of four because there are four hotplates, then wire it through to the griller and into the stove element where it will be stored in microwave proof cake containers to keep it fresh and crispy... until we need it. When we have enough we will send it out via the frypan.
Mess:	But wait, master. What about Superperson? He will suspect if he senses the draining of the power of the universe and come looking for us.

Pong:	I was wondering when you'd spot that problem. I have a plan for Superperson.
Mess:	You have, master?
Pong:	What is it that will attract Superperson to this corner of the universe?
Mess:	Free style and blow wave?
Pong:	No.
Mess:	Discount on superhero costume dry cleaning?
Pong:	No. Think, fool. What is it that would get any red-blooded male really going?
Mess:	Bran Pops, master?
Pong:	Women, you fool.
Mess:	Women? Never heard of that breakfast cereal. Is that the one *(insert the name of youth group leader)* likes?
Pong:	Probably. But enough. We'll capture that dumb big-eyed blonde he's always rescuing. The one who keeps fainting.
Mess:	The one with low blood pressure.
Pong:	We'll use her as bait, and when golden boy comes to rescue her... whammm!
Mess:	But how, master? We don't know where she is.
Pong:	Oh, she always drops in just about when we need her.
	(Sound effect: bell rings twice. AMELIA NICE enters.)
Amelia Nice:	Shop, service, hello... you have a customer.
Pong:	Quickly, it's her. We must mix some concoction to knock her out. Get some of the knockout juice I keep for when the mother-in-law visits.
Mess:	Yes, master. *(Quickly runs around to gather ingredients as PONG names them.)*
Pong:	Sodium curare, nicotine, aspirin, monosodium glutamate to bring out the flavour, wheat germ for healthy skin, morphine for sweet dreams, and three drops of... *(Insert name of minister.)* hair restorer.
Mess:	What does that do, master?
Pong:	Nothing. It just adds texture.
Mess:	*(Panting and out of breath.)* Here it is, master.
Pong:	This will really knock her out.
	(Both come out to where AMELIA NICE is standing waiting.)
Amelia Nice:	Oh, it's you. I think I'm going to... *(She faints.)*
	(MESS looks at the mixture and sobs with disappointment, then places it on table. PONG and MESS both pick up AMELIA NICE and tie her to a chair.)

Amelia Nice: *(Reviving.)* Oh, what's happening? Oh, you two. Just wait. I'll call Super-person and you'll be in trouble.

Pong: Scream along, baby. We'll even help.

Mess: Yes, because when he comes we'll be ready for him.

Amelia Nice: *(Screaming.)* Help! Who will rescue me? Is there no one to save me?

(SUPERPERSON enters as theme music plays.)

Superperson: *(Yells to audience.)* Hi, kids!!! *(Turning to AMELIA NICE.)* Fear not, Amelia Nice. I picked up your cries for help on my shriek-o-phone. It registered 9.5 on the Richter scale.

Amelia Nice: Your heard my screams, then?

Superperson: The whole cosmos heard your screaming. Who is responsible for holding you like this? Aha!

Pong: Ah, Superperson. This time we have you. You will not escape.

Superperson: No, you don't have me, my friend, because I represent kindness and niceness and all that soppy stuff, and I am going to thrash you. But first, a cup of coffee. *(Picks up the cup containing the drug.)*

Amelia Nice: No, Superperson, no! Don't drink it.

Superperson: It's all right. I can take it without sugar.

Amelia Nice: No, don't... It's not coffee, you big hunk, you great gorgeous guy, you stupid great clod, idiot, moron.

Superperson: Tastes like... mmmmmm. *(Takes up stance of a gridiron player.)* Well, you two, prepare yourselves for a thrashing. Now, 41 22 hike. *(Goes through a drawn-out fainting routine.)* That stuff has a real belt to it.

Amelia Nice: Oh, Superperson... what have they done to you?

Pong: He's out to it. Tie him up quick.

(They tie him to a chair.)

Now to my machine and the ultimate control of the universe. Mess, turn on the stove. Set the plates at five. Rotisserie on. Watch over the wok. I'll put the oven on 365 degrees.

Mess: Yes, master. I feel the power coming through. What will we do with it?

Pong: Let's destroy a planet. What's that pitiful planet there? Earth. Focus the power on it. Let's have some fun. Ha ha. All the power in the universe is mine to do with as I please.

Superperson: *(Reviving.)* You'll never get away with this, Pong. What do you think, Amelia?

Amelia Nice: I think I'm going to...

Superperson: Yes. Going to faint. I know.

Mess: Master, something's wrong. The dials on the stove are turning themselves off.

Pong: What? That's not possible.

Mess: Master, the power is surging. I can't control it. The rotisserie is turning too fast. It's out of control.

(A sign appears, saying "Boom!")

Master, it says "Boom".

Pong: Drat. It must have blown up.

(They throw themselves backwards.)

Yes, it did.

(Message appears: "You didn't really think you could control me, did you?")

Mess: Look, master. It's flashing a message.

Pong: But who? Who speaks to Emperor Pong in this way? How can an inanimate power source speak?

Mess: What's "inanimate", master?

Pong: It means it doesn't have a brain. Just like you.

Mess: Is that an insult?

Superperson: You fool, Pong. You've lost.

Amelia Nice: Yeah.

Superperson: You cannot presume to control for yourself the ultimate power of the universe.

Amelia Nice: Yeah.

Superperson: You cannot use it...

Amelia Nice: Yeah.

Superperson: ... because that power is...

Amelia Nice: Yeah.

Superperson: Shut up—you're ruining my speech. That power is a person. He's not going to allow himself to be used.

Amelia Nice: He's going to flash up a message saying "Push off". One... two... three.

(Nothing appears on the screen.)

Pong: See, there's no personality there.

(Message appears: "I do things in my own time.")

Great chunks of chow mein!

Mess: We didn't realise what we were dealing with. We'd better get out or we'll be stir fried.

(They both exit quickly. As they go, SUPERPERSON boos them. Still tied to their chairs, SUPERPERSON and AMELIA NICE stand.)

Superperson: Well, guess I handled that. Got you out of that one, Lord.

Amelia Nice: Oh, Superperson, now you can rescue me and take me out. Get me out of this.

Superperson: Of course. Er, Lord, how's about getting these ropes off. One... two... three.

(Message appears: "You know I don't work like that.")

Oh yeah. Heh heh heh. It goes to show you, you cannot expect God always to get you out of all your little predicaments. You have to accept the consequences.

Amelia Nice: Superperson.

Superperson: Yes?

Amelia Nice: Shut up and get me out of this.

Superperson: Er yes, of course. No problems. I'll get you out and take you out. Perhaps we could take these chairs with us and save booking a seat.

Amelia Nice: Oh, Superperson, you're so clever.

Superperson: Yeah.

(They struggle out as the lights fade and the "Superperson" theme plays.)

BIBLE READINGS

Romans 1:18-23
Job, chapters 40 and 42.

QUESTIONS FOR DISCUSSION

1. Make a list of ways in which the power of God is evident in the universe.

2. How do we try to influence God to our own designs?

3. Does God answer our prayers? All of them? Should we always expect an answer?

4. Are there things you would never pray for? If so, what and why not?

5. When have you prayed and received an answer different from the one you expected or hoped for? How did you feel?

6. What experiences have you had where God gave you what you needed rather than what you wanted?

THE GREAT OFFICE SWINDLE

CHARACTERS

Richard Tracery
Norm Christian
Various offstage voices

SCENE: *The stage is divided in two. On stage right is the office of RICHARD TRACERY, private eye. It consists of a desk with a light over it (optional) and a chair. On stage left is NORM CHRISTIAN's office, comprising a desk/table and chair. All other office features are incorporated in mime sequences. Onstage action alternates between stage right and stage left, with no link between the two. Make this separation clear by using lights to light each side of the stage in turn, or have each actor freeze while the other is acting. First focus on stage right. RICHARD TRACERY enters.*

Richard: Hi, Richard Tracery here. Private nose... public nose... private road... public bar... never mind! I'm one of those people who snoop around. I was in my office reviewing some confidential files with my secretary...

(Offstage: loud feminine giggle.)

... when I took a fall...

(Offstage: loud strangled cry... "Aagghhhhhhhhhh".

I'll try that again. I took a call. It was to be my toughest case ever. It involved embezzlement, corruption and graft at the highest level. It was... the Great Office Swindle.

8.45 The call came through. A major metropolitan company was suffering a massive fall in profits. Prelimary research had been undertaken by the police graft squad, but they couldn't uncover anything. No money was actually being taken. It was obviously a brilliant mind at work, using devious white collar and computer criminal networks. The commissioner called me to his office.

9.01 I left my office. Couldn't help thinking I'd forgotten something.

9.02 I fell down the stairs.

9.04 Returned to office to put clothes on.

9.23 I arrived at the specified place. It looked like an ordinary twenty storey office building, except for the unit of armed police on guard. Those boys shoot first and ask questions later. *(Looks at a point offstage and speaks in this direction, changing voice as if talking to a group of police.)* Morning, boys.

(Sound effect of machine gun fire.)

Policeman: *(Offstage.)* Are you Richard Tracery?

Richard: *(Speaking to audience.)* I told you they shoot first and ask questions later. I was ushered into the commissioner's office.

Commissioner: *(Offstage—voice is loud and gruff.)* Sit down or I'll slap you down.

Richard: *(Speaking to offstage.)* Yes sir, Mr Commissioner. *(To audience.)* He briefed me as to the case, the details and the requirements.

Commissioner: *(Offstage.)* Get the criminal!!!!!

Richard: *(Speaking to offstage.)* Yes sir, Mr Commissioner. *(To audience.)* And I was ushered out. *(Throws himself across stage to indicate how he was ushered out. Speaks to offstage.)* Thank you, Mr Commissioner, thank you. *(To audience.)* I sped to the scene of the crime and infiltrated the inner office inconspicuously. Cleverly disguising myself as a potted palm I installed myself in a prominent hallway. From there I made the following observations.

Monday, 9.30 a.m. Enter Norm Christian, half an hour late.

(Lights fade on RICHARD TRACERY. Focus changes to stage left. Enter NORM CHRISTIAN, looking around.)

Norm Christian: Darn, it's nine thirty. I'm half an hour late. But I couldn't help sleeping in after spending all day yesterday organising the fellowship supper. I'd better sign on. *(Mimes signing the register.)* Now I must brighten up someone's day. Aha. A "God loves you and so do I" sticker will help people when they sign the attendance book. *(Sticks sticker down.)* Gee whiz, it went over my clock-in time and reason for being late. Oh well, it may save a soul.

(NORM CHRISTIAN looks around and whistles loudly as he walks off. Focus changes to stage right and RICHARD TRACERY.)

Richard: This could be my man. I made a note on one of my leaves to keep watching him.

10.05 A lady came in with her pet poodle. Make a note to have potted palm suit dry cleaned.

10.30 I was witness to one of the greatest ripoff rackets the world has ever seen. The venue? The cafe bar machine and the office biscuit tin.

(Change focus to stage left as NORM CHRISTIAN enters.)

Norm Christian: Ah, coffee. Nothing like it. Oh... that's what I forgot. I was supposed to get coffee for the fellowship coffee shop. I'll never make it to the shops in time. Aha! *(Looks around.)* They'll never miss a tin or two, and a few packets of biscuits. I'll replace them later, if I remember.

(Walks off, whistling loudly. Focus changes to stage right and RICHARD TRACERY.)

Richard: This was my man all right. In spite of his loudly professed religious leanings, this man was a master criminal. As I watched, amazed, he revealed more and more aspects of his kleptomaniac character and his devious crimes.

11.45 a.m. On an assignment for the boss to get a new box of paper clips from the office stationery room, he returned with paper clips plus...

(Focus changes to stage left. Enter NORM CHRISTIAN.)

Norm Christian: Wow!!! Look at all this butchers paper and crayons. Just what I need for my Sunday school lesson this week. And glue. I need a new bottle of that too, for their models of Zacchaeus in the tree. They'll never miss all this stuff—it's been here for years. I can put it to good use. Hey, there's a phone too. As long as there's no one else around... *(Dials a number.)* Hello, Pearl, a line out please. Yes, it's a business matter. Oh, hello, George, about the youth group outing this month—could you drive the fellowship mini-bus...

(Focus changes to stage right and RICHARD TRACERY.)

Richard: The guy was a genius. He was running at least six rackets at once. What do you think, Bumbles?

(Offstage voice mumbling.)

That's what I was going to say.

3.30 After lunch, which included one hour eating and one hour's prayer and meditation, he was assigned to file some confidential material on the highest shelf, with the help of Miss Freelove the secretary. She was voluptuous and well endowed in every way, with beautiful hair, clear blue eyes and great legs. Of course, I took no notice of this.

(Focus changes to stage left and NORM CHRISTIAN.)

Norm Christian: Er... Miss Freelove, you climb up the ladder and I'll hand these heavy files up to you.

(Mimes looking up at her on top of the ladder. Focus changes to stage right and RICHARD TRACERY.)

Richard: And later in the day, yet another monstrous ripoff. Time 4.00 p.m. Venue—the photocopy machine.

(Focus changes to stage left and NORM CHRISTIAN.)

Norm Christian: Oh look—the photocopy machine and no one else around. Well, I've got to copy a couple of documents, so while I'm at it I'll do a couple of copies of the chorus book for this weekend's Sunday school picnic. Now all the children will be able to sing the choruses. What a worthy cause. *(Feels in pocket.)* Darn, no change. I'll pay for them later probably. Oh, look at the time. It's four forty-five. Only fifteen minutes to go. May as well go now.

(Whistles loudly as he goes off. Focus changes to stage right and RICHARD TRACERY.)

Richard: And that's how it went—day in, day out. I observed whistling boy all week. His other crimes are as follows. He listens to Christian music with a headphone set while working. He unfortunately did this while working on the end of month bank reconciliation statements and mucked them up, forcing a review of the entire accounting system.
An examination of the attendance book showed two days "sickie" taken because he was tired out after a secondary school camp.

He ruined several important files by placing "God loves you" stickers all over them.

He caused widespread frustration throughout the office by writing religious messages on other people's blotters.

He even went as far as posting religious tracts under toilet doors.

Finally, when the supervisor confronted him about his inefficiency and told him, "You better straighten up, loony, or you're out", he replied, "I forgive you for abusing me", and walked off.

My reckoning showed that he did approximately five hours of work per week. Then he collected his cheque for forty hours on pay day. But what a brilliant cover-up for a master criminal. Who would suspect that this loudly professed, evangelistic man, heavily involved in church and community work, was responsible for the massive losses incurred by this company?

Immediate arrest was the only answer for this man. It was an open and shut case. We had him cold. I called the commissioner and got an arrest warrant. Then I left my desk, put on my coat and checked my service revolver. Quickly I made my way to the office of whistling boy. He wasn't to be a free bird for long. I got in the lift and pushed the up button. Looking at my watch I noticed it was four forty-five. Only fifteen minutes to go. May as well go now. I pushed the down button. It was time to knock off. It had been a hard day. Wadda you say, Bumbles?

Bumbles: (*Offstage.*) Mumble... mumble... mumble... beach.

Richard: Yeh, I was thinking of going there too.

Bumbles: (*Offstage.*) Mumble... mumble... mumble... women.

Richard: Yeh, I know.

Bumbles: (*Offstage.*) Mumble... mumble... mumble... drinkies.

Richard: Yeh, that too. Let's go.

(*Lights fade or curtain closes.*)

BIBLE READINGS

James 2:14-26
James 1:8

QUESTIONS FOR DISCUSSION

1. How did Norm shape up as a Christian? In what ways did he show his faith? In what ways did his actions belie it?

2. Make a list of ways in which people's actions may not match their faith.

3. Each of the things that Norm Christian ripped off is only small in value. Do they really matter? Why?

4. Do you think good intentions can sometimes justify dishonest actions? (Give examples.)

5. Should a Christian be perfectly behaved every day? Do we use our humanity as a cop out?

6. What would you like to say to Norm Christian in a discussion about Christian faith and witness?

© 1990 THE JOINT BOARD OF CHRISTIAN EDUCATION
The Divine Sticky Stuff: 20 short plays for churches
by Chris Chapman, Susan Chapman, Peter Gregory and Heather Allison

OUT OF HAND

CHARACTERS

Professor Time-Bender
Woman
Man
Offstage voice

SCENE: *Curtain opens to reveal a bus stop seat down stage centre, desk and chair stage left, and desk and chair stage right. There can also be a stool down stage right for Professor Time-Bender to sit on as he narrates. The stage is divided so the action involving the MAN, the WOMAN and PROFESSOR TIME-BENDER can be lit independently (or those not involved in the action can freeze). PROFESSOR TIME-BENDER enters.*

Time-Bender: Hi, I'm Professor Heatherington Smyth Time-Bender. Today we look at a common social phenomenon. Through seeing these everyday situations we can find out how to meet and make friends. Then we can learn how to make better friendships for ourselves. The situation we will look at today is meeting people at the bus stop. Let's see how it goes. Action please.

(MAN and WOMAN walk from opposite sides to centre stage where there is a seat. They sit down and wait. Bus comes as indicated by their eyes and gestures. They both stand up and bump each other; the WOMAN drops her handbag. They each blame the other, refuse to apologise, and walk off after a brief verbal confrontation. Needs to be brief.)

Time-Bender: An unfortunate incident, to be sure. But never mind, perhaps they'll be able to patch up and make up. We'll take my little time machine here and go two years into the future to see.

(PROFESSOR TIME-BENDER presses button on calculator-sized machine and lights flicker and fade for a few seconds while a weird sound like a machine noise or similar provides audio effect. When lights come up, the MAN and the WOMAN are sitting at separate tables on opposite sides of stage. Each is speaking into a telephone. Focus on MAN.)

Man: *(Gossip-type conversation slandering woman about the behaviour of her children.)*

(Focus changes to WOMAN.)

Woman: *(Gossip-conversation about a supposed affair the man is involved in.)*

(Focus changes to PROFESSOR TIME-BENDER.)

Time-Bender: Well, it doesn't look as if they're back together as friends yet. In fact, they seem to be conducting a little slander campaign against each other. But I don't think this will go very far. After all, they are adults. Let's warp time again and see what's going on a couple more years from now.

(Presses time machine button again and the light/sound effect comes over. Focus changes to MAN.)

Man: *(Telephoning again.)* And I'll tell you another thing. You know that woman I can't stand? Well, I found out it was her who's been spreading the gossip about me all this time, so I got her back. Don't know why I didn't do it years ago when the whole thing started. I put a slow burning fuse in the fuel lines of her car— that big one she likes to drive around.

(Focus changes to WOMAN.)

Woman: *(Talking on telephone.)* ... so I thought to myself, that would be just like him to spread that sort of gossip round about my kids. No wonder they wouldn't give Jimmy that job when he left school. So you know what I did? I put a really hot love letter from some non-existent woman into his letter box. Wait till his wife finds out. That will be the end of their marriage. Hold on... I can smell something burning.

(Focus changes to PROFESSOR TIME-BENDER.)

Time-Bender: Well, we seem to be getting out of hand here. But surely they can forgive and forget. I mean, it was such a little incident at the bus stop. Let's go on another five years.

(Presses time machine button again and the light/sound effect comes over. Focus changes to WOMAN.)

Woman: *(Talking on telephone.)* Look, I don't care how you do it, but I want that march broken up and good. Get a few dozen of your boys into that black tenement area on Fourth Avenue. Tell 'em lies, tell 'em anything, but get 'em stirred up good. Take a few boxes of those concealable pistols with you too...

(Fade lights or all freeze as loud newscast type music plays over.)

Voice off: Here is the news. Riot police and Special Branch personnel were called into action today on Fourth and Fifth Avenues when a series of running street battles broke out between ALR supporters and Liberty Party protest marchers. The army was called in after police using water cannon and tear gas failed to disperse the mob which official estimates put at well over 10,000. Sporadic fighting is continuing into the night and the sector has been closed off...

(Voice and music fade. Lights up on PROFESSOR TIME-BENDER again.)

Time-Bender: Isn't it amazing how these things get out of hand? What's going on five years later? Dare we look?

(Time travel effect again. Desks and phones again, but now characters are in miliary uniform. Maps etc on desks. Focus on MAN.)

Man: *(Talking on telephone.)* Listen to me. I've been at this command post ever since the civil war started, and I know what I'm talking about. I don't see any logistical problems. I want that tank squadron in sector 34 and fast. It's the only weak point in the line. Can't they understand that?

(Focus changes to WOMAN.)

Woman: *(Talking on telephone.)* I don't care if I am the only woman commander on the western side. I say we are making rapid progress in that area—the first big headway we've made since the city split up—and I want to take advantage of it. What about the air wing? Can't they give us any support? I don't care what the United Nations do. Their peace force will never be here in time.

(Lights fade on all as sound effects of war come over, if possible teamed with a rear projection screen display of rapidly sequenced war shots from Vietnam, Cambodia, etc. Sound effects need to be really loud and well done or they'll sound corny. Effects fade after about eight seconds. Focus on MAN.)

Man: *(Talking on telephone.)* I'm not listening to any more of her proposals. We've had nothing but treachery from them all along. And besides, it looks as if the U.S.A. may be going to side with them. The time for strong action is now. I'm going to press the button and wipe them all out.

(MAN freezes, his hand about to push the button. Lights stay on him, and also come up on WOMAN.)

Woman: *(Talking on telephone.)* They have broken the ceasefire once too often. I'm tired of waiting for him to negotiate—and anyway, the Russians are showing him too much sympathy for my liking. It's time for the final solution.

(They both push the button on their desks. Immediately all lights go out. A massive explosion rumbles through while rear projection screen shows a glowing red fireball in the sky. When lights come up again there is only a single spot on PROFESSOR TIME-BENDER. Desks are empty; chairs upturned.)

Time-Bender: Far-fetched? Maybe. But when you think about it, people are bumping into each other every day. And wars are happening every day too. No wonder Paul says, "Don't let the sun go down on your anger". Perhaps instead of fuelling our anger with hatred and revenge we should all learn a lesson from the way God forgives us... Well, now it's back to... *(Insert current year.)* ... to start again.

(Presses time machine button and the time machine audio/visual effects come back again. Stage full light as MAN and WOMAN walk on to bus stop and sit down exactly as before. Bus comes and they stand and bump into each other again, but this time they freeze as they look at each other so no one knows what the reaction is going to be.)

Time-Bender: Well, what do we do now?

(Blackout and curtain.)

BIBLE READINGS

Ephesians 4:26
Romans 1:28-32
Matthew 6:14-15
Mark 11:26
Matthew 18:21-35

QUESTIONS FOR DISCUSSION

1. As the situation in this play worsens, each party becomes more determined to win and less likely to admit fault. How does this relate to Romans 1:28-32? How can we avoid it happening in our own lives?

2. Think of examples where small differences left unchecked have developed into major rifts.

3. What is the central issue that causes these problems to snowball?

4. If you had to isolate one sin as the major cause for unrest in our world today, what would you choose?

5. What do you do when your offer of forgiveness or attempt at reconciliation is rejected by the other party?

PETER

THE SOCIETY BOX DOLL

CHARACTERS

Dr Frankenernest
Nurse 1
Nurse 2
Society Box Doll
Igor
Offstage voice

SCENE: *The curtains open on a dimly lit stage. On stage right there is a riser with a chair on it. Under the chair is a black box. Down stage centre is a table with two books on it.*

Voice off: Scene: the inside of a ruined and isolated castle, somewhere in the dark Transylvanian woods. The sky is black and ominous. A flicker here and there illuminates the cliffs and casts long shadows.

(Someone backstage throws some tin cans across the floor.)

The wind rustles in the trees. "Russell, get out of that tree."

(Sound of several wolf howls.)

Er, sound man, can you do something about that feedback in the system, please?

(Lights come up on stage and two NURSES enter from stage left. They are cleaning their fingernails and chattering.)

Nurse 1: He's a strange man, the doctor. A genius, but strange.

Nurse 2: Why do you say that?

Nurse 1: Oh, I don't know. Just a few little things that I can't put my finger on.

Nurse 2: You mean the rats. But all these old castles have rats in them.

Nurse 1: Yes, but most people don't dress them in bonnets and tuck them into bed.

Nurse 2: Yes, that's true. Then there's the chandeliers of course.

Nurse 1: Most people don't swing on them while chanting their shopping list.

(IGOR sneaks into the room with an axe. He is a hideously ugly creature, who walks bent nearly double. He straightens up and towers over the two nurses and howls.)

Nurse 2: Oh Igor, you're such a bore.

Nurse 1: Yes, Igor, you really are getting a little dull.

Igor: *(Obviously upset.)* Didn't I even scare you a little bit?

Nurse 1: No, you didn't. Now go away.

Igor:	I'm a failure. I can't scare anyone. Like those people I tried to scare last week. They all laughed at me and one of them dropped my axe on my big toe.
Nurse 1:	Now now, it was a very tough kindergarten you went to last week.
Nurse 2:	Yes. Now that I think about it, you did scare us a little bit. *(Looks to other nurse to support her.)*
Nurse 1:	Oh yes, I certainly was scared. Very good, Igor.
Igor:	Do you really mean it?
Nurse 2:	Yes. By the way, the doctor's coming.
Igor:	Not **the** doctor?
Nurse 1:	Yes, him!!!!
Igor:	There must be something big going on.
	(A long, drawn out scream comes from offstage. It sounds like someone talking.)
Nurse 1:	It's in the top drawer near the handkerchiefs, dear.
Nurse 2:	*(Gasp.)* I think I hear something. It must be him.
Igor:	Not the doctor.
Nurse 2:	Yes, it's him.
	(IGOR tiptoes to up stage and hides. DR FRANKENERNEST enters. IGOR comes out from hiding to scare the doctor by creeping up behind him. Doctor swings around unexpectedly on IGOR and shouts "Boo!!!" and Igor falls to the ground in fright.)
Doctor:	Oh Igor, I'm such a kidder.
Igor:	Please don't ever do that again, master.
Doctor:	Right, Igor, first things first. I've perfected the straight ray machine.
Nurse 1:	The straight ray?
Nurse 2:	The straight ray?
Igor:	The straight ray!!?
All:	What's the straight ray?
Doctor:	A ray to make you straight again, Igor. It's taken years to perfect and it will only work once, so if you're ready...
Igor:	Straightness. I'll be tall again. Oh, goody.
	(DR FRANKENERNEST brings out a ray gun and shoots it at IGOR, with appropriate sound effects. IGOR slowly straightens up and stands tall.)
	Yahoo! I'm straight again. I'll never be laughed at again.
Doctor:	Good on you, Igor, tallness is yours again.
	(DR FRANKENERNEST claps IGOR on the back in congratulation and IGOR hunches back over again.)

<table>
<tr><td></td><td>Oh well, never mind. I like you better that way.</td></tr>
<tr><td>Nurse 1:</td><td>And what do we do today, doctor?</td></tr>
<tr><td>Doctor:</td><td>We test my most amazing invention. It's the most amazing, incredible, unbelievable thing ever created.</td></tr>
<tr><td>Nurse 2:</td><td>The Uniting Church? (Or insert name of the local church youth group.)</td></tr>
<tr><td>Doctor:</td><td>No, not that amazing. It's this. (Pulls out the black box from the riser and extends the antenna.)</td></tr>
<tr><td>Igor:</td><td>You invented the radio, master? We listen to loud rock and roll music. (Begins to sing.)</td></tr>
<tr><td>Doctor:</td><td>No, Igor. (He moves to sit in the chair on the riser.) Today we test our perfect human being. The one we created last week after years of intensive research and back-breaking work.</td></tr>
<tr><td>Nurse 2:</td><td>You mean the one we sent away to Marvel Comics for?</td></tr>
<tr><td>Doctor:</td><td>Quiet—you're ruining the effect. For years we have worked to create the perfect human, but all our early models have failed. They look human but they're not. They're a social failure because they don't know how to behave. Their actions are completely misguided. Even my last model was hopeless... a slob... it goes on rampages at the slightest provocation. It's a foul horrible sight. Its teeth glinting in the moonlight, it stalks poor innocent creatures. It's got horrible smelly breath and its speech is barely intelligible. This creature has no idea at all how to behave in public. It's a menace.</td></tr>
<tr><td>Igor:</td><td>The incredible hulk?</td></tr>
<tr><td>Doctor:</td><td>No, it's... (Insert name of local youth group leader.) We can't go on producing these failures. We can't find any more room for them in... (Insert name of your home town.) We've got to succeed with this model. We must give it a decent standard of behaviour.</td></tr>
<tr><td>Igor:</td><td>Shall I bring in the new model, master?</td></tr>
<tr><td>Doctor:</td><td>Yes, Igor, bring her in. Throw the switch.</td></tr>
<tr><td></td><td>(IGOR rips a switch off the black box and throws it.)</td></tr>
<tr><td>Igor:</td><td>Master, I think I did a very bad thing.</td></tr>
<tr><td>Doctor:</td><td>You're a dull boy, Igor. What are you?</td></tr>
<tr><td>Igor:</td><td>A dull boy, Igor.</td></tr>
<tr><td>Doctor:</td><td>Give that thing to the nurses.</td></tr>
<tr><td>Nurse 1:</td><td>Idiot.</td></tr>
<tr><td>Nurse 2:</td><td>Moron.</td></tr>
<tr><td></td><td>(IGOR growls at them and towers over them with his hands raised. The NURSES tickle him under the armpits and he collapses to the floor giggling.)</td></tr>
<tr><td>Doctor:</td><td>When you've finished, Igor, we'll get on with the experiment. Now, that little black box you are holding is very important because it tells our new</td></tr>
</table>

perfect human being how to behave. It gives her standards to live by. Bring her in now.

(The NURSES help the DOLL in as they control her movements with the box. DOLL walks like a wind-up toy and stands rigidly.)

Let's look at the instruction manual and try a few basic reactions. Igor, go and stand by her.

(IGOR moves over by the DOLL and stands staring at her.)

Right, firstly we'll try excitement. You're going to the movies tonight. Press the red button.

(DOLL goes into wild paroxysms of delight and crawls all over IGOR. Then stops suddenly, going rigid.)

Let's try passion. That's the switch on the left.

(The DOLL begins to passionately embrace IGOR. Then stops as before.)

Anger.

(DOLL animates again and thumps IGOR.)

Igor: Just like a woman. First they love you, then they hate you.

Doctor: Sadness.

(DOLL begins to weep on IGOR's shoulder. Then stops.)

Igor: Too late for apologies now, sweetheart.

Doctor: Fear.

(DOLL goes into a wild panic and then leaps into IGOR's arms.)

Well, they seem to be the normal reactions. Let's try some basic social situations. The society box will tell her how to act. Let's try the sophisticated party situation.

Doll: *(Talking in a false upper class English accent. Very rich and very spoilt.)* Oh, hello there, darlings. How nice it is to see you after all this time. What a bore this weather is. I mean, how can one expect to get a good tan with so much cloud about? I don't know, really. I mean, life is just one tragedy after another. First Jeremy gets worms and has to be clipped, but the salon won't be open until Tuesday and even then we can't get an appointment until 3 p.m. But Jeremy is bearing up well—he's a good little dog. But if that's not enough, there's no caviar for dinner and we have to watch the black and white TV in the Rolls because the colour is on the blink. Oh dear me.

Doctor: Now, how would she act with the tough street corner types she hangs around with after work?

Doll: *(Talking like a street gang member.)* Right, all youse idiots, whadda ya want? You think you're tough? Well my mum's so tough, she doesn't wash dishes, she eats 'em. And you—yeah, you—what you laughin' at, eh? You think I'm funny or sumthin'? 'Ow would you like to be wearin' your nose on the other side of your face? I'm so tough I can spit in the street and everything, and smoke and get lung cancer if I want, so there. And who are you to tell me what to do? I don't take orders from no one, muscle brain. *(DOLL goes rigid again.)*

Nurse 1: She seems a little schizophrenic, doctor.

Nurse 2: She's got too many standards of behaviour to conform to.

Doctor: Well, that's the society box standard. She's got a set of behaviours for every occasion. Now we'll try her at church and teaching Sunday school.

Doll: *(Bending over as if talking to children.)* Now, children, the Good Samaritan took the poor man to the inn and told the innkeeper to look after him until he was well. So, children, this story tells us to be kind to those people who are in trouble. That means when you see that little boy with the buck teeth and glasses down the back of the school, you don't go down and beat the snot out of him. You go and put your arm around him and be his buddy— even though you think he's smelly. *(Goes rigid.)*

Doctor: Now let's try at home with mumsy and dadsy.

Doll: *(Animating again)* Oh, you wouldn't understand about my problems. You just don't care. I have to go to school, you know. What do you do all day? Go to work, don't you, and earn money? And what do you give me? A mere $15 a week. What sort of allowance is that to give a kid who wants to go out and enjoy life? And what about Errol? You hate Errol, don't you? I can see it in your eyes every time he comes over. What's wrong with 11,000 cc Harley Davidsons anyway? Just because he's got a few tattoos you hate him. You're prejudiced, that's what you are. Bigots. Why don't you join the National Front? But you don't care about me. What about my problems? I went to school the other day and my pencil broke, but do I complain? **Nooo!** You just hate me. *(Goes rigid again.)*

Igor: *(Looking at shiny antenna.)* Hey, I like that bit.

Doctor: No, don't! *(Runs to stop IGOR ripping out the antenna, but is too late.)*

Nurse 1: Idiot.

Nurse 2: Moron.

(IGOR prepares to menace them with a howl, but the NURSES howl at him first. He jumps back in fright.)

Doctor: You've broken the Society Box. Now what's she going to do? It gives her the standards she lives by. Now she's got nothing to tell her how to behave. She won't know how to act. She could do anything.

Igor: Look, master, she's moving.

Nurse 1: What's she going to do?

Doctor: I don't know—but under the circumstances, I think it would be better if **you** went and handled this situation.

Nurse 1: **Me!?**

Doctor:	**Go!** Or I'll short out your brain circuits and give you a headache. *(NURSE 1 goes over to DOLL, who is fully mobile now, but disoriented.)*
Doll:	Oh hello, isn't it a lovely day? I had a wonderful time at school.
Nurse 1:	That's good. Do you feel better now?
Doll:	*(Speaking in changing voices.)* Yes, well I... no I'm not, you stupid old bat. Watch out or I'll...
Nurse 1:	Well, have it your own way, sweetie! *(Retreats.)*
Doll:	*(With erratic actions and changing voice.)* Don't you sweetie me, or else... I say, isn't that pretty... how about a bottle of grog? Haven't any of youse got some... and so you see I've just come back from Sunday school and little Jamie Cuthberson... burn the whole place down, man, and then we'll get the motor bikes and find a few straights and... mix me a cocktail, waiter... isn't it about time for a cup of tea?
Nurse 2:	She seems to be a bit mixed up.
Doll:	How about we get all our... *(Insert name of current rock group.)* records and play them at 6 million decibels and blast this corny establishment apart and then get the heroin and... some Mozart and Brahms might be nice, too, and we could... and that, children, was how David defeated Goliath and... come on, baby, light my fire. Take me home to your pad and I don't care. Gee, I like your car... this is the sixth annual report of the church committee and dear old Mrs Barlow... got rotten drunk last night and was falling over everything and got into this huge brawl... don't know what's going to happen to the garden... *(Goes tense and freezes.)*
Doctor:	Something's gonna explode. She doesn't know what to do without the pressures of the Society Box to tell her how to act.
Nurse 1:	But can't you do something?
Nurse 2:	She may be dangerous.
Doctor:	She will be.
Igor:	Master, she's moving. She's coming this way. I want my mummy.
Doctor:	You can't have your mummy. I sent her back to Egypt.
	(DOLL advances, threateningly.)
	Quick, Igor, get the instruction manual.
	(NURSE 1 and NURSE 2 are now hiding behind DR FRANENERNEST.)
	Read something from it to see if she recognises it.
Doll:	All right, you guys, this is it... don't see what there is to be afraid of... I'm gunna kill ya...
Igor:	I can't read, master. Here, try this. *(Hands DR FRANKENERNEST a Bible.)*
Doctor:	That's not an instruction manual, Igor.
Igor:	Read it anyway, master. It might work.

Nurse: Read it. Read it.

Doctor: "His weak, human body died on the cross, but he now lives by the mighty power of God. We, too, are weak in our bodies as he was, but now we live and are strong, as he is, and have all of God's power to use in dealing with you." Aw, that's no good.

Nurse 1: Doctor, look!

Nurse 2: She's slowed down. She's thinking about it.

Igor: Read more, master.

Doctor: "I have been crucified with Christ and I myself no longer live, but Christ lives in me. And the real life I have now in this body is the result of my trusting in the son of God, who loved me and gave himself for me."

Doll: *(Beginning to understand.)* Thank you. I feel better now. I feel like a real person. Well, goodbye. Can't stay—I must tell other people.

Doctor: Hey, where are you going? You just can't walk out of here like that. You can't defy the Society Box. It's the only thing that tells you what to do.

Doll: No, I've found a better standard now. I don't need that pressure any more. I'm free of it. 'Bye. *(Exits.)*

Doctor: But you can't defy the standards of society. They tell us all what to do. Igor, tell her that she can't defy society.

Igor: Shut up, master. I'm reading here about someone who did.

(DR FRANKENERNEST and NURSES gather around IGOR, who is reading the Bible. Lights dim and curtains close.)

BIBLE READINGS

Matthew 6:24-26
James 4:4
Romans 12:2

QUESTIONS FOR DISCUSSION

1. What kinds of pressures are on us to act in certain ways? To what extent do non-Christian values determine our actions?

2. Read Matthew 6:24-26. To what masters other than money do we surrender?

3. In which areas would you expect a significant difference in priorities between a non-Christian and a Christian?

4. How does Romans 12:2 relate to this drama?

© 1990 THE JOINT BOARD OF CHRISTIAN EDUCATION
The Divine Sticky Stuff: 20 short plays for churches
by Chris Chapman, Susan Chapman, Peter Gregory and Heather Allison

A HISTORY OF THE WORLD

CHARACTERS

Cave people
Peasant 1
Peasant 2
Peasant 3
Scientist 1
Scientist 2
Scientist 3
Professor
Interjector

SCENE: *The stage is divided into two centres of action. Each side of the stage should be lit independently. The PROFESSOR enters, stage left.*

Professor: Good evening. Tonight we discuss the history of the world, right from the start of everything. In the beginning, the world was made by God, and he made all the animals and stars and fields and rocks and all that's in it, and then he made the human race— males and sheilas. He made all human people, and then he made... *(Insert the name of a well known person.)*, and it's never been the same since.

But let us transport ourselves back to those first early days of the human race... the primitive peoples who roamed the earth in small groups and tribes, hunting and gathering, back in the infancy of man...

(Sound effect of babies crying.)

Stupid boy! To enable us to explore this ancient era more closely, let us travel back in time with the aid of my newest invention: the Time Bender. It also doubles as a toaster, you know. *(Holds up toaster for audience to see.)* Now, let us go back in time to the shores of a lake in Kenya, to the earliest traces of man, and we see a small band of primitives, sitting around a fire, roasting Papa Luigi's pizza.

(Lights on other side of stage, illuminating the group of CAVE PEOPLE.)

Life was harsh for these people. They had to rely on their wits and brains, and that's why life was harsh. But they had hands, with separate digits, fingers, finely tuned instruments of work, able to be used for the great discoveries that would shape history.

(One of the CAVE PEOPLE picks nose.)

And here, also, we see the development of ideas.

(CAVE PEOPLE follow actions as he speaks.)

Man reaches his penultimate level of development as he discusses and implements new ideas which shape the course of history. Here is a leader among the group. A thinker with a new idea. He is presenting his new, revolutionary idea to the group. He is determined to lift them out of the mire of their harsh way of life. Change, progress, is in the air as he speaks. The others recognise a new idea. They see it is different from that which they already know... and... they... beat the heck out of him. And that's what often happens. Now, let us journey forward in time to the middle ages...

(CAVE PEOPLE exit, dragging their victim. Light fades as PROFESSOR pushes a button on his Time Bender. There is a brief sound effect appropriate to the Time Bender and the light comes up again to reveal a group of medieval PEASANTS.)

Here, peasants labour under a feudal society, where nobles and aristocrats exploit them and live a life of luxury and satisfaction. Some poor peasants were kept working in the fields, day after day, for nothing. No money, cruel task masters over them, beating them and whipping them. They must have been working for... *(Insert name of minister of local youth group.)*

(PROFESSOR walks over to speak to PEASANTS.)

I'd like to ask you a few questions. *(Holds up note book.)* Er, what are your ideas on God?

Peasant 1:	God? Aghh! Flee from his wrath! Lightning bolts! Repent, everyone, repent!
Peasant 2:	Whip yourselves, quick, or be judged! Don't bring plagues on us, Lord.
Peasant 3:	Wait on! God is love. The Bible says so. He is just and loving. He doesn't want to hurt us. He wants to be friends with us.
Peasant 1:	This is a new idea. God is love?
Peasant 2:	Friends with us?
Peasant 1:	No more whipping. *(Pauses to think.)*
Peasant 2:	Heretic!
Peasant 1:	Witch! You're a witch, aren't you?
Peasant 2:	Burn him! *(Ruckus of yelling: "Burn... witch... heretic.")*
Professor:	Wait on... wait on... why do you want to burn him?
Peasant 1:	Because he's thinking differently from us.
Peasant 2:	And we don't like it. *(Pause.)* Hey, wait on. Speaking of witches, where did you come from?
Professor:	I'm a time traveller, from far in the future.
Peasant 1:	Time traveller, eh?
Peasant 2:	Then you're a witch too.
All:	Burn, burn, burn...
Peasant 1:	Attack the intruder, brothers.

(The mood of PEASANTS 1 and 2 turns ugly and they begin to get aggressive. PROFESSOR steps back in fear and then pushes the button on the Time Bender. To simulate the PROFESSOR being carried away in time, the PEASANTS can move offstage backwards while still yelling and waving threateningly. Light fades as PROFESSOR moves back to his original position.)

Professor: Getting all rather familiar, isn't it? Well, now we go into the present day, the twentieth century, the age of science, technology, knowledge and enlightenment. Ever since the Renaissance and the Industrial Revolution, man has charted a course of astounding progress through his technological discoveries. He has been to the moon. He has explored the depths of the oceans and the earth's surface. Things are clearer now than they have ever been. Certainly we have problems, but the old attitudes of the dark and ignorant past have surely been improved and modified into a new awareness and an open-minded approach, no?

(Light fades as he pushed the button on the Time Bender and comes up on the other side again showing three SCIENTISTS. PROFESSOR moves into light and approaches them.)

Professor: Er, excuse me.

Scientist 1: Excuse... excuse... Analyse the word, quick.

Scientist 2: Excuse... a commonly used polite expression meaning a plea for relief from duty or to be allowed to leave an assembly, etc.

Scientist: Put it under the microscope, quick.

Scientist 2: Dissect it.

Professor: Er, I only meant... excuse me. Here, have a jelly baby.

Scientist 1: *(Grabs the jelly baby from PROFESSOR.)* Jelly baby... a small sugar-based sweet popular with younger children.

Scientist 2: Coloured confectionary based on sugar, water, gelatine and food colouring prescribed by the Health Regulations Act.

Professor: Er, gentlemen, what are your ideas on God?

Scientist 1: God? Tripe, rubbish, mythological concept of primitive people to explain natural phenomena they don't understand.

Scientist 2: Psychological projection from man himself to relieve feelings of guilt and insecurity.

Scientist 3: No, wait on. God is a person. He really exists, and he is loving, just, helpful and creative.

(SCIENTISTS 1 and 2 look at each other for a second and them explode with anger.)

Scientist 1: Idiot. Primitive fool!

Scientist 2: You unsound psychological upstart!

(Both rave at him about evolution, proof and psychology. PROFESSOR pushes the button on the Time Bender and leaves them raving. Fade lights and bring up again on PROFESSOR as he enters opposite side of stage again.)

Professor: And so it goes to show that whatever you see in the history of the world, there are always two things to notice. People don't like ideas that differ from their own, even if they're right. And people are afraid to stand against public opinion—and everyone bashes them up if they do. How ignorant. I'm glad I'm not like that.

Interjector: *(From audience.)* I disagree with everything you've said so far.

(PROFESSOR pulls out gun and shoots INTERJECTOR.)

Professor: Good evening.

BIBLE READINGS

Hebrews 11:36-37
Matthew 11:16-19
2 Timothy 3:12
John 15:20
Acts, chapters 5, 6, 7, 8

QUESTIONS FOR DISCUSSION

1. Why do people tend to persecute anyone who is different?

2. Should Christians be significantly different from non-Christians? In what way?

3. Have you ever undergone persecution because you are a Christian? Give examples.

4. It has been said that if you're not persecuted you aren't making your Christianity public enough. Do you agree with this statement? Why?

5. Can a Christian "enjoy" persecution in an unhealthy way?

6. "A Christian life should be a joyful life even under difficulties." Discuss what we have to be joyful about.

7. Compared to some Christians in other countries, do we really suffer *any* persecution?

© 1990 THE JOINT BOARD OF CHRISTIAN EDUCATION
The Divine Sticky Stuff: 20 short plays for churches
by Chris Chapman, Susan Chapman, Peter Gregory and Heather Allison

THE SUPER SALESPERSON

CHARACTERS

Customer
Super Salesperson

SCENE:	*Opens with the CUSTOMER sitting doing a crossword puzzle.*
Customer:	Now let's see. Four across, a three letter word starting with C that means automobile. Now what can that be? Better get the dictionary. Where is that dictionary?
	(SALESPERSON enters quickly.)
Salesperson:	Hi! I heard you call.
Customer:	What?
Salesperson:	I'm Ace Simple from the Acne Computer Company, and boy, have I the computer for you!
Customer:	But I don't need a computer. I've been working on my crossword. A dictionary will be perfectly adequate.
Salesperson:	No no. Rubbish. You need **this**. Our newest machine. It can decipher the meaning of any words. This is the 640k RAM Custard Apple II micro word cruncher.
Customer:	But I don't need it.
Salesperson:	Yes you do. This will increase your word deciphering capabilities by 10,000 times. All you need is this one inexpensive unit. Plug right in and you're away.
Customer:	But there's no screen. I won't be able to see what I'm typing.
Salesperson:	Well, you can plug it into your colour TV and you'll be able to see it all. You'll need to buy one of our RF modulators, of course.
Customer:	Colour TV? I've only got a black and white.
Salesperson:	You haven't got a colour TV? Boy, are you in luck. You see, we have heaps of them in our big liquidation sale. "Big Luigi" has over-ordered and everything has to go.
Customer:	That's okay then.
Salesperson:	Of course, you'll need our patented software package that runs the computer. However, you have to buy a licence that entitles you to legally use the program. And if you buy the licence very soon you will receive a 100% discount... Oh sorry! You didn't do it soon enough—but you do get a free chook.
Customer:	But I don't want a free chook.

Salesperson: However, there is one little flaw here. There is no actual power supply, and you have to add one yourself. Now, we do have a special nickel cadmium battery that we sell, or if not, our company also markets a special electric line adaptor which is plugged into a generator that you hire at a special rate from Ripoff Hire Service. But you only get the special rate if you join the Custard Apple Club. Now, if you buy this whole package, you win not only a free chook, but your name goes into the barrel and you could be the lucky winner of a trip for two to Hawaii, the Solomon Islands and three nights in Hollywood, all expenses and accommodation paid by you.

Customer: What about the runners up?

Salesperson: They get a chook, free. And now, to print the results of your program, you need this... 600 character per second light sensitive graphics line printer used by NASA to design the last space shuttle operations. Pity about that... and it's going cheap.

Customer: But I only want to find the answer to this crossword clue.

Salesperson: But it'll do your whole crossword in Old English script with cute little borders around the edge. And, if you buy it all before yesterday, you win the chance to buy a chook. Of course, there is also the all-inclusive insurance policy required, which is valid only if you purchase our fire extinguisher and asbestos blanket... and our fire extinguisher and asbestos blanket insurance policies. And what happens if you want to have a shower or go "toy-toy" during the cold long nights when you're using all this equipment? Then all of this can be neatly packaged for you in one of these fantastic Cosy-Nook Mobile Homes produced by our company, which also produces the V-8, 4-wheel drive, off-road truck you'll need to tow it. And, with each truck sold, a free chook on ten days approval. If, after ten days, you can still stand it, you can eat it. Our company also markets clothes pegs. Now, for the lucky millionth customer...

Customer: Aren't you getting a bit out of hand?

Salesperson: Yes, but once I get going, I can't stop.

Customer: But all you started selling me was one little computer, and you put in all this extra unnecessary garbage.

Salesperson: What are you trying to do, put me out of a job or something?

Customer: No, but all I want is something simple. Just something to help me understand the meaning of words.

Salesperson: Well, why didn't you say so? Why don't you just get a dictionary?

Customer: Oh yeah, never thought of that...

Salesperson: But while I'm here, we do have this great plan for a leather bound, 54 volume dictionary with lots of...

(Fade sound and light. Curtain.)

BIBLE READINGS

Isaiah 56:11-12
Luke 12:15-20

QUESTIONS FOR DISCUSSION

1. How can we avoid being overwhelmed by modern technology?

2. In what ways do advertisements play on our greed for more material goods?

3. "Enough is enough." What **is** enough?

4. Why do political leaders and others keep talking about raising our standard of living? Is there a limit to how high our living standard can go? How will we know if and when we reach the limit? What then?

5. Is greed a problem largely for western nations, or for the whole of humanity?

THE CELESTIAL MESSENGER BOY

CHARACTER

Celestial Messenger Boy

SCENE: *MESSENGER BOY enters carrying a small knapsack.*

Messenger: Oh boy, what a day! It's a real job keeping up with all these chores.

Being the celestial messenger boy is no joke, you know. There's so much to do. I should apply for a few cherubs to help me. Already I've had to tune all the harps and lyres of the entire angelic host, fluff out the clouds, polish the pearly gates, and clean and sharpen the swords of the armies of heaven. Then there's all the others to do: polish the streets of gold, spray the andromeda constellation with Spray and Gleam to add more shine and sparkle. Phew! In heaven, every day seems like an eternity.

Now, what do I get onto next? I've got all these secret confidential papers to deliver to the heavenly Auditor General. I must deliver them as soon as possible, so here's the celestial salute... *(Salutes.)* Neither rain nor snow nor dark of night shall keep me from my appointed duty. *(A beeping sound is heard, as if from a wrist watch.)* Doesn't say anything about morning tea, though. *(Sits and unpacks knapsack.)*

Now, what's mum given me today? More pure white chocolate *(Or insert the name of a local sweet related to the stars.)* Oh no, not that again... angel food cake! *(Tosses it aside.)* What's this? *(Gasp!!!)* Devilled ham paste sandwiches! Back! Back! *(Fights the sandwiches and beats them into submission.)*

Now... *(Takes out bundles of letters.)* What's this I've been given? *(Reads.)* "Top secret. Highly confidential. For the Auditor General only." *(Drops them.)* Good heavens! They've fallen to the ground. *(Opens bundle.)* Heavens above! The impact of the fall has burst them open. I'd better check and see if they're all still in order. Now, what's this?

Hmmm. It's a letter. Hey, these must be the requisitions for goods and services that have been sent up from earth. Hey, here's a list of requests from the people of... *(Insert the name of your country.)* There's a request here from a woman who wants a second car so she doesn't have to walk to the bus stop when her husband has the... *(Insert the name of a popular brand car.)* Poor woman.

Here's one from a union that wants a nine-day fortnight with increased wages and company paid holiday plane flights—all because they say they've got increased work stress and work load.

Here's another one from a man who wants a dishwasher so he can watch TV instead of doing the dishes. He's sent a letter. It says: "Can I also have another colour TV so the kids can use the portable? After all, charity begins at home and everyone is always talking about peace. Well, this will make peace in my small corner—and every little bit helps. And could the colour TV have a video game attachment please?"

Here's one from a school kid: "Dear God, my mother keeps making me sandwiches for lunch, but I want to buy my lunch like all the other kids so I just throw the sandwiches in the bin. Can I have extra pocket money so I can buy burgers each day?" Yeah... I sympathise, kid. No more angel food cake, mum. Gee. These people live under a lot of stress. Modern living is full of hassles— such a fast pace of living, emotionally draining... inflation and all that.

Look. Here's another bundle of letters. Wonder where this comes from. It's postmarked... Somalia *(Or subsitute the name of another Third World country which has been in the news recently)*. *(Opens one and reads.)* Gee, what a come down! This one starts off: "Help! Will someone please hear this. The Red Cross doctor is writing this for me because we cannot read or write. We have many problems, but please could we have rice for our children? Our cattle have died in the drought and the soldiers have come and taken away our pigs and chickens. We cannot bear to hear our children crying with hunger. I cannot bear to sit with my wife and watch our baby dying. Please send us food for one more week—and peace, so we can farm our land again."

Gee whiz! *(Still reading, almost ashamedly, picks up the lunch he threw aside before.)* Here's another one: "Please tell the rich countries about us. They mustn't know about us, because no one is coming to help us. Please let them send us help so we can grow our crops... to heal our sick, and to stop the floods that wash our land and fields away."

Look at this one from a kid who can't read and wants to go to school... *(Looks at bundle.)* Gee, there are thousands of them. What is the Auditor General going to do? I'd better get these in fast. *(Gets up to go with the bundles of letters, one in each hand.)* Gee, if he's got so many from the poor countries, why bother with these? *(Tosses rich letters aside.)*

(The MESSENGER BOY gathers up his things and walks off stage.)

BIBLE READINGS

2 Corinthians 11:24-29
Galatians 6:2

QUESTIONS FOR DISCUSSION

1. The message here is very obvious. Can you think of some of your own problems which seem small compared to those of others?

2. What types of people are most prone to continual complaining?

3. List ways in which we can keep a realistic view of the world situation and maintain an accurate perspective of our own problems.

4. List the things the people in the Third World requested. How many times have you complained about those very things? Give specific examples.

5. Helping others can help you keep your feet on the ground. How?

6. Can you think of any other characters in history who have endured more than we have for the faith?

© 1990 THE JOINT BOARD OF CHRISTIAN EDUCATION
The Divine Sticky Stuff: 20 short plays for churches
by Chris Chapman, Susan Chapman, Peter Gregory and Heather Allison

YOU ARE THE MAN

CHARACTERS

Woman
Man
God (offstage voice)
Tough guys

SCENE:	*The scene opens with two characters on stage. The WOMAN is very angry with the MAN.*
Woman:	And another thing, ugly. Don't you ever, ever dare to come near my house again, you pointy-nosed freak! I never want to see you again, so there! *(She blows a raspberry at him and stalks off.)*
Man:	Oh yeah? Well, you'll be back. You'll see.
Woman:	Won't.
Man:	Yes you will. *(Sits down.)* She'll be back. See if she isn't. Boy, you can't win...
	(WOMAN comes back.)
	See. I told you you'd be back.
Woman:	I forgot something.
Man:	Yeah?
	(WOMAN slaps him across the face.)
Woman:	That was what I forgot. *(Storms off stage.)*
Man:	Boy, how do you like that? First she lies to me, then insults me. None of it was my fault. Misinterprets everything I say. Then hits me and stalks off. Wow. Women. *(Sits down.)* This world is really going to the pack. There's weirdos all over the place. You can't get away from them. The whole joint is going down the drain. Why doesn't God do something about it? Boy, if I was him, would I ever straighten a few people out!
God:	*(Offstage.)* Such as who, for instance?
Man:	Huh?
God:	Such as who?
Man:	Who's that?
God:	It's me—God. You were just wishing you were me so you could fix the world up a bit.
Man:	God?
God:	Yes. You know—the guy in charge. So who do you want to straighten out?
Man:	I'm talking to God?

God:	My boy, you talk to me every night before you go to sleep.
Man:	You listen to that??
God:	Yes, I listen—but I can never get a word in edgeways. You're always asleep before I can say anything.
Man:	Oh.
God:	So who do you want to straighten out? Name any three types of people who bug you and I'll punish them.
Man:	Really?
God:	Yep.
Man:	Oh boy. This is a dream come true. Now let me see. Who can I get? Wow. The range is endless. Who really annoys me? Some mean rotten ugly... *(Insert name of local youth group leader.)* The name just jumps at you! No, I can do better than that. Let's think.
God:	Hurry up. I'm busy, you know. There's lots of work to be done at... *(Insert name of neighbouring town or suburb.)* ...and I have to check through... *(Insert name of local personality.)* 's account books.
Man:	Liars! They really get me. All the political con men and big-time advertising jive talkers ripping off the poor common man and always getting away with it. I wish... I wish three of the toughest street fighters in the world would visit every one of them and beat the heck out of them.
God:	Very well. Who else?
Man:	And insulting big mouths. They turn me off too. All those really big put-down artists and gossip column writers and mudslingers always insulting people and dragging them down. Yuk! I want you to get a 100 kilogram weight and drop it on the head of every one of them.
God:	Okay then. The last lot? Who are they?
Man:	Thieves. All those corrupt officials in governments around the world who steal millions every day. And big-time corporations who dodge tax, and people who steal from others and muck their lives up. They're the worst. I want... hee hee... I want each one tickled to within an inch of his life, all the time being shocked with 450 volts of electricity. Oh, that would be great!
God:	Is that all?
Man:	Yep. That's it.
God:	Very well, then. *(Sound of quiet laughter.)*
Man:	What's so funny?
God:	Oh, just a little private joke of mine.
Man:	I didn't realise you had a sense of humour.

God:	Of course I have a sense of humour. Otherwise I wouldn't have created... *(Insert name of local church celebrity who can take a joke.)* Here goes, then... Liars first, wasn't it? With the street fighters.
Man:	Yeah. Hee hee. Oh boy, is this going to be good! Are you ready, all you dishonest creeps? Here it comes. Go to it, Lord!
	(Lights dim if possible. Three TOUGH GUYS rush in from different points around the stage. Kick the MAN around and then exit as the lights come up. The MAN picks himself up and shakes his head as if in a daze.)
	Hey, what is this, man? You crazy or something?
God:	Well, you said all liars.
Man:	Yeah man, but I'm no liar.
God;	What about that day when you told your boss that you were sick when you were really at the beach?
Man:	Ah, man! I mean big-time liars—international crooks and con men.
God:	Yes, they all got it too. But a lie is a lie. Now, who is next?
Man:	Oh well. I suppose it was worth it just to hear the screams of the next mob, the big mouths. One... two... three... go to it, Lord—a hundred kilograms on each big inflated head!
	(A "weight" drops on the MAN, or is thrown in from offstage. A carton painted black with 100 kg painted on it in white does the job. The MAN picks himself up dazedly.)
	Hey look, Lord, this is getting a bit rough!
God:	There are dozens of times I have seen you insult and put down people.
Man:	I do not, ya big... oops!
God:	Now for the last lot... the thieves, I think. Didn't you include an extra apple in that dozen you bought the other day?
Man:	Yeah, but I mean the big-time crooks, loan sharks and real estate ripoff artists—organised crime and that.
God:	Yes, they'll get it too. But a theft is a theft, big or small, and that makes you a thief too. You've condemned yourself. There's nothing I can do about it. Now, let me see... tickling, wasn't it?
Man:	Oh now, wait a minute, Lord... have a heart!
God:	And the electric shocks.
Man:	Oh no, you wouldn't...
God:	You pronounced the punishment. This is all your idea.
Man:	Oh no! Get away... stop it!

(*MAN goes into writhing hysterics. There is a loud hum from offstage or over the sound system, and he screams "Ooooooooo" as if in pain—then continues the hysterical laughter and begging for mercy as the curtain closes.*)

BIBLE READINGS

Romans 2:1-6
Matthew 7:3-4

QUESTIONS FOR DISCUSSION

1. Do you think God was too hard on the man?

2. Why do people find it so difficult to admit their own faults?

3. How often do we hide behind excuses rather than face a situation realistically? Give examples where this has happened to you?

4. What can we do about those people who **are** big-time bad guys, causing more pain, death and poverty than most average people ever will?

5. Is one sin or one sinner worse than another—or is the only real issue that all have sinned?

THE REAL PERSON

CHARACTERS

Adolescent girl
Athlete
Student
Voice over

SCENE: *Before lights come up or curtain opens or any characters enter, hair-style advertisment music plays. Lights come up on stage to reveal a teenage GIRL seated, speaking on phone. Music fades.*

Girl: To the dance? Me? Oh John, do you mean it? Thanks. Yes. At eight o'clock. 'Bye. *(Hangs up phone and freezes.)*

Voice over: Only three weeks ago, this girl found it so difficult to talk to boys. She was lonely, rejected, until she discovered...

(Advertisement music for clothes shops, perfumes, hair salons, etc. plays over as GIRL dances confidently around, displaying clothing and hairdo. The music can be effectively provided by a chorus of voices offstage singing with gusto the punchlines from a few well-known ads. As music fades the GIRL goes back to phone and dials.)

Girl: Hi, Julie, it's me. Guess what. Johnny asked me out. Yes, it's true. The jeans, makeup, hairdo, cologne water, lipstick, underwear and body-wave worked. I'm a real person, just like the ones on the ad. *(Replaces phone and minces happily off stage.)*

(As GIRL disappears, VOICE OVER of second ad comes and ATHLETE dressed in tracksuit or other athletic gear enters, working out with callisthenics or dumbbells.)

Voice over: Were you always the butt of school jokes? Did you have sand kicked in your face? What did it do for your self-respect? Build yourself up, using our scientific processes, to the shape you want to be. Increase your confidence and self esteem. You'll win the admiration and respect of others too, and become a real person, at Hercules Super Gym.

Athlete: *(With a very thick "dull" accent.)* At Hercules Super Gym they built up my ... body. Me and my friends all go there. There's a lot of weights and dumbbells there. *(Exits singing an appropriate song to himself. From offstage comes a thump.)*

Athlete: *(Offstage.)* Hey, one of my biceps fell off.

(School STUDENT in uniform comes on, rehearsing or reading class morning talk.)

Student: Morning, Miss Whackford, girls and boys. My talk is on my hobby which is music. I collect lots of records and I have a big hi-fi set. It's a Prickle A49

Ultra-Sonic model. It has 200 RMS watts per channel, 40 centimetre woofers, 15 centimetre squawker, 7 centimetre tweeter. It's got a ten slide graphic equaliser and a digital tape deck. It's got a direct drive turntable and a phase lock loop and it came with a free chook. Not only that, but I got the full *(Insert the name of a popular group here and where the * appears below.)* collection including their latest preview single, and all the * singles.

I got an original factory copy of the first * track and the lead singer personally autographed it. Well, he didn't actually sign it—he spat on it—but that's the same thing. And I've got two tapes I illegally made at the * concert. I even got the latest album by the *(Insert the name of local choir group here.)*— it's got a record cover and a free frisbee inside. And I got my * shirt, and my * hat and my * boots, and right now I'm saving for a triple Prickle Quadra-sonic compact disc set. Then it'll be the ultimate. People will like me and want to come round to my place and everything. I'll be a real person. That concludes my morning talk.

(STUDENT exits. Multi-coloured light effects on stage with down tempo, slow dance, nightclub music. Couple stroll sophisticatedly across stage.)

Voice over: Come on down to Sweet Talkin' for the best music in *(Insert the name of your town here.)* This is the place for you. We'll get you in, we'll make you move, we'll show you a good time till 3.00 a.m. And the drinks just keep on flowing. After dancing, come on up to the Dome room and relax. Take in the video clips or the laser light show. Just the place for a quiet drink or smoke. This is the Sweet Talkin' Club. A new dimension in night life.

BIBLE READING

Matthew 23:27-28

QUESTIONS FOR DISCUSSION

1. Why is it considered so important to be good-looking or self-confident or popular?

2. What makes a person "successful"?

3. Many gimmicks claim to offer solutions to people's problems and hangups. What are some that you have encountered? What did they promise? What did they deliver?

4. What is your idea of a "real person"? How does a person become "real"?

THE DEVIL AND DUDLEY

CHARACTERS

Devil
Dudley Christian
Jesus

SCENE:	*Curtain opens, or lights come up on DUDLEY at his devotions, seated or kneeling. Alternatively, he can enter and begin.*
Dudley:	Lord, thank you for this time of quiet prayer to you in this nice church building. I pray that this week you will free me from temptation in all its forms and allow me to live a pure and blessed life. Lots of love, your loyal servant, Dudley Christian. *(Begins to sing a chorus or hymn.)*
	(The DEVIL, very smoothly dressed and wearing sunglasses, enters silently and perches himself at DUDLEY'S elbow.)
Devil:	Hello, Dudley.
Dudley:	Oh hello. Who are you? I don't remember seeing you in this church before.
Devil:	No, I don't attend church regularly—that is, unless I have a special reason.
Dudley:	I see. What's your name?
Devil:	Devil.
Dudley:	Oh, that's a nice name. Devil who?
Devil:	Oh, that's actually my second name.
Dudley:	Oh. What's your first name?
Devil:	The.
Dudley:	The Devil. **The Devil!** You are **the** Devil? **The** Devil?
Devil:	*(Coming intimidatingly close.)* Of course. Don't you recognise me, Dudley? You are quite an old friend of mine. We go back a long way.
Dudley:	*(Terrified at the prospect.)* A long way?
Devil:	Yes, Dudley. You're one of my regulars.
Dudley:	Regulars?
Devil:	Yes. *(Suddenly changing sides and popping round Dudley's other cheek.)* Remember the sickie you took off work last week?
Dudley:	But...
Devil:	Well, who do you think gave you the idea?
Dudley:	Save me, Lord.

Devil:	What about the two dozen red pencils you stole from work the other day to take home for your little brother to colour in with, eh?
Dudley:	Shhh. This is a church.
Devil:	I know, Dudley. But who cares. As long as I'm around, you don't get much say in things, so it doesn't matter who you are. *(He begins to poke, bullyingly, at Dudley.)* You're a real pushover, Dudley.
Dudley:	Help me, Lord. Save me.
Devil:	Why do you think they call you **Dudley**?
Dudley:	Save me, Jesus. Take this temptation away.
Devil:	*(Soft sell over now, he begins to shake DUDLEY roughly.)* So let's get down to business, Dudley. What about the money you handle at work? No one checks up on it.
Dudley:	*(Trembling.)* No.
Devil:	Couldn't you use a bit of it to help pay off your car?
Dudley:	Yes, I could. I mean... help me, Lord.
	(JESUS enters and stands quietly.)
Devil:	Oh Dudley, don't come on with all that religious guff. Why not give in? It'll probably hurt a lot less!
Dudley:	Lord, save me.
Devil:	He's not coming, Dudley. Funny, you're doing all the right things. But anyway, I guess Jesus doesn't care about you any more, you mealy-mouthed little wart! So come along with me, and we'll have a good time.
Dudley:	Jesus. Save meee!
Devil:	Oh Dudley, you silly boy. What's Jesus ever done for you? He's nothing but an ineffective weakling, just like you.
	(Suddenly, at the name of JESUS being insulted, something happens inside DUD-LEY.)
Dudley:	*(Gasp.)* Jesus! A weakling? Now listen here, Mr Beelzebub...
Devil:	Dudley, I don't like that name.
Dudley:	Oh yeah? Well cop this, Mr Beelzebub. The Lord Jesus happens to be my best friend, and he helps me.
Devil:	Oh rubbish, Dudley!
Dudley:	*(Fuming, leaps with rage and waves fingers in the air.)* It's **not rubbish**! It's true! And he gives me strength. And with his strength I can defeat you, Mr Beelzebub.
Devil:	Dudley, watch the suit. *(But he is back-stepping and uncertain, and it is now DUDLEY who is poking him around.)*

Dudley: *(Poking harder and harder.)* So you'd better take a walk, my friend. Back to the fiery furnace and toast your tuxedo down there, because the power of the Lord Jesus is going to iron you out good and proper!

(By this time DUDLEY has poked the DEVIL across the stage to the wings. With a final shove he sends the DEVIL toppling, screaming offstage, and apparently down into the pit.)

Dudley: *(Puff, pant.)* He's gone. It worked!

Jesus: Hello, Dudley.

Dudley: Oh Jesus. You're here.

Jesus: Of course I'm here. I've been here for ages. You called me some time ago.

Dudley: Well, now that you mention it, yes, I did. Why didn't you save me when I called? Why did you let me get pushed around like that for so long?

Jesus: I was waiting to see you fight.

(DUDLEY looks at JESUS, puzzled for a second. JESUS laughs and punches him lightly on the shoulder. DUDLEY realises that he has done the right thing and becomes more pleased with the situation.)

Dudley: Hey, you're right. I **did** fight.

(They begin to exit, talking.)

Jesus: You did well.

Dudley: Couldn't have done it without you.

Jesus: No, but you stood up to him well.

(Talking fades as lights or curtains are brought down, or characters just exit, still talking.)

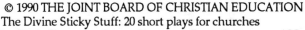

BIBLE READINGS

Matthew 4:1-11
1 Corinthians 10:13
Hebrews 2:18
Hebrews 4:15

QUESTIONS FOR DISCUSSION

1. The Devil came to tempt Jesus after Jesus had spent forty days in the desert. What do you think Jesus might have been doing in all this time alone?

2. How did Jesus deal with each temptation? Are there any common features in the way he dealt with them all?

3. Read the Hebrews passages again. Do these verses change the way you see Jesus as relating to you, and his ability to answer your prayers?

4. What excuses do we put up to cover our failure to deal with temptation? How valid are they?

5. Can we sometimes expect Jesus do "do all the work" in our spiritual lives?

6. "God helps those who help themselves." How true is this old saying?

ESCAPE FROM GOD

CHARACTERS

Adam
Eve
Jonah
Moses
Commentator 1
Commentator 2
Voice of God
Enid
Elijah

SCENE: *Sports music plays as COMMENTATORS 1 and 2 enter and sit at desk down stage centre.*

Commentator 1: Good afternoon, ladies and gentlemen. Here we are at the *(local name)* stadium for the first running of the Escape and Hide from God Marathon. Earlier heats have gone very well with some fine competition, but the field has been narrowed down from the original four billion to these final competitors. The athletes will be coming into the stadium any time now, and each is determined to escape and hide from God.

(ADAM and EVE enter.)

Here are our first two athletes—Adam and Eve—the only married partner team left in the field. *(To COMMENTATOR 2.)* Over to you.

Commentator 2: These two have really been training hard for this event. They've been on a strict vegetarian diet and this has really promoted their level of fitness.

(ADAM and EVE, who have been warming up side stage, now approach to be interviewed.)

Adam and Eve, I believe you've been on a special diet in preparation for this event.

Adam: Yes, we've been on a strict fruit and vegetable diet.

Eve: Especially the fruit part.

Commentator 2: I understand you also have a strong motive to want to win this race.

Adam: Yes, we need to escape from God because we have a lot of explaining to do about our diet recently.

Eve: Especially the fruit part.

Adam: So we need to win.

Commentator 2: Thank you, Adam and Eve.

(COMMENTATORS can call for audience applause if they wish. It is a good audience participation point.)

And back to you now.

Commentator 1: You can hear the roar of the crowd as the next competitor enters. It's Moses. Known as the Boy from the Bulrushes, Moses is an experienced escaper. He's been training a lot lately, running up and down pyramids and beating up Egyptian slave masters.

Commentator 2: Moses, I understand you've been on the run a lot lately.

Moses: Yes, that's right. I've been on the run mainly from the Egyptian police, and I want to put up a tough opposition to anyone else in this event because I've also got to escape the responsibility of leading the Israelite slaves out of Egypt.

Commentator 2: Thank you, Moses.

Commentator 1: A great favourite with the crowds, now—we have Elijah.

(ELIJAH enters.)

Commentator 2: Elijah, why do you want to escape and hide so much?

Elijah: Well, Queen Jezebel's after me for a start, and she's wiped out most of the true prophets and I'm next on the hit list. I'm sick of being a prophet for the Lord. I can't handle the pressure any more. It's all too much, so I've decided to get out while I can.

Commentator 2: Thank you, and good luck.

Commentator 1: Finally, we have the ultimate escaper—Jonah.

(JONAH enters.)

Commentator 2: Jonah, how confident do you feel today?

Jonah: Quite confident, thank you. I've got some really great hidey holes sorted out, and there's no way the Lord's going to find me and make me go and preach to the people of Nineveh. No way!

Commentator 2: Have you been doing any special training?

Jonah: Yes. I've been on a seafood diet, and I've been doing a lot of swimming. Just had a thought that it might be handy, you know.

(JONAH lines up with the other atheletes.)

Commentator 2: Well, what with these competitors in the field, I think the audience is in for some pretty exciting escaping and hiding today.

Commentator 1: Yes, sir. Now, for those unfamiliar with the rules of this event—all these individuals have special tasks to do for the Lord, and they want to get out of them. The competitors are given a certain amount of time to escape and hide from the Lord anywhere in the world, and then the Lord has to find them. The Lord is an experienced finder, so it should be an interesting event.

Commentator 2: The winner is, of course, the person who isn't found by the end of the day—and that person gets to escape from the tasks and responsibilities that the Lord has planned for them. *(Goes to start the race.)*

Commentator 1: Well, all the athletes are in place and the starter is ready. Quiet in the stadium, please.

Commentator 2: Take your marks... get set... go!

(All the athletes run screaming in various directions. Lights fade to darkness as athletes conceal themselves on various parts of the stage or in the audience.)

God voice: 1... 2... 3... 4... 5... 6... 7... 8... 9... 10... Coming, ready or not. *(Single tight spot comes up and roves stage until it lights on MOSES, sitting covering his eyes.)* Moses! *(MOSES leaps up and races off stage. Spot roves again and picks up ELIJAH tippy-toeing across upstage.)* Elijah? *(ELIJAH races off in panic. Others are similarly discovered fairly quickly, and all race off.)* Boy, these humans certainly can be silly. *(Lights up again.)*

Commentator 1: Well, the first bit of action has gone off nicely. The athletes will need a bit of time to establish their hiding places.

Commentator 2: We'll be back right after this commercial break.

(Optional break here. Action resumes as ENID enters, dressed in apron with feather duster. Furniture may have been rearranged to demonstrate a new setting.)

Enid: Oh well, another day, another dollar. Life's pretty tough when you run the motel at the end of the universe. We get all sorts in these out of the way places, and they're usually on the run from someone. But you don't get many legitimate customers here at the end of the universe. Last lot was a nice group of... *(Insert some local or other group who have been in the news lately for questionable activities.)* ...but they left in a hurry. Well, what's the work list for today? I've got to dust out the honey jar, put blue flush in the letter box, deodorise the television set. I've hardly got time to scratch meself—and would you believe it, Meals With Wheels rang up the other day and asked me if I could help. *(Laughs. ADAM and EVE enter surreptitiously.)* Oh look—customers.

Adam: Hello. My name's... er... Smith. This is my wife... er... Mrs Smith.

Eve: Yes. Mrs Smith.

Adam: We'd like a room, please.

Eve: Lots of privacy. No messages. No visitors. No one will ever find us here.

Adam: No one need know we're here at all.

Enid: Of course. No need to be embarrassed. We have lots of newly-weds here. So from now on, mum's the word. Lunch will be in two hours. It's pork chops with apple sauce, followed by apple crumble and apple juice.

(ADAM and EVE have been looking progressively sicker as this list is read out.)

Adam: Oh... er...

Eve:	We'll just have a cup of tea, thank you.
	(They rush off as MOSES enters cautiously.)
Enid:	Morning, sir. A room?
Moses:	Er... yes, please. No visitors. Completely private and no one need know I'm here. Got it?
Enid:	Certainly, sir.
Moses:	There's only one thing I want. I want a room with a bed that's shaped like a giant basket. You see, I've got a thing about baskets. Can't sleep unless I'm in one. Don't know where I got it from.
Enid:	A basket? Well, I'm sure we can hunt something up, sir. Room 2.
Moses:	Thank you. *(Rushes off.)*
Enid:	Basket, eh? I wonder if my old laundry basket would...
Moses:	*(Rushing in again.)* Er, I wonder if I might remove something from my room. It's a... well... it's a large potted plant, a bush in a pot.
Enid:	Yes, sir. We have plants in our rooms, sir. It's healthy.
Moses:	Well, could I stand it in the hall or something? You see, I've got a thing about bushes. Don't know what it is. They're a fire hazard. That's what worries me.
Enid:	Certainly, sir.
Moses:	Thank you.
	(MOSES exits. ELIJAH enters.)
Enid:	Morning, sir. A room? With lots of privacy and no visitors?
Elijah:	Yes. Exactly.
Enid:	Any special extras?
Elijah:	Er... yes actually.
Enid:	Here we go.
Elijah:	I'd like my meals brought up to my room, please.
Enid:	At last—a rational request. Room service. How would you like them brought up, sir?
Elijah:	By a raven.
Enid:	A raven?
Elijah:	Yes. You see, I've got a thing about ravens.
Enid:	Well, I've got a few chooks out the back. I could spray paint a few of them black and send them up with the tray.
Elijah:	Fine. Thank you.
	(ELIJAH rushes out, muttering that he'll never be found. JONAH enters.)

Jonah:	Hello. Do you have a room with a large aquarium in it?
Enid:	Yes, sir. Room 4 has a large aquarium.
Jonah:	Good. I'll take it.
Enid:	Room 4?
Jonah:	No, the aquarium. I... er... like sleeping in them, you know. It's a thing I have about them.
Enid:	*(Really worried by this last one.)* Yes, sir. Yes, sir. It's all right. The guppies will just have to move over.
Jonah:	Great. They'll never get me here.
	(JONAH races out. There is a pause. ENID looks round to see they are all gone, and then glances upwards.)
Enid:	They're all in, Lord.
God:	Thank you, Enid. I'll handle it from here. Come out, come out, wherever you are! *(All athletes race in from various points, gibbering in panic.)* All right, all right. You've been found. Stop running around. *(They settle down.)* Don't you feel ashamed of yourselves? *(They all nod.)* You can't hide from me, can you? *(They all shake their heads.)*
Adam:	But we've got to get away from you, because we can't look after the whole garden and obey all the rules too.
Eve:	Yeah, the snake made us do it. Blame him.
Moses:	I can't lead the people of Israel out of Egypt. I'm not a good speaker, and anyway... they'll never believe me.
Elijah:	And I can't keep going as a prophet. I'm the last of the lot and I can't take the pressure any more.
Jonah:	And I can't preach to the people of Nineveh. They'll skin me alive. They like doing that to people, you know—and I don't want to waste this tan.
	(General rabble of objections, which ends on a predetermined signal.)
All:	Why can't someone else do it?
God:	Because each one of you has been chosen carefully according to my plan, and has been allotted a special task which only he or she can do. You and everyone else in the world have a particular job to do—and if you don't do it, there will be a task left undone.
Moses:	But what can one do against so many?
God:	By yourself, nothing. That's why I'm going to help you.
Moses:	Oh well, that's different. Why didn't you mention it before?
God:	I **did** mention it before. Read Exodus 3:12, when you eventually write it.
Moses:	How can I argue with that?

God: Now go, all of you, to the tasks I have selected for you. And remember—I will be with you all the way.

(Athletes look at each other in an encouraged fashion and all exit, possibly singing some well known march tune or appropriate popular song about getting on with it.)

Enid: *(Clapping and cheering them on.)* Go on... off you go. Things will be tough, but they'll work out. You heard what the Lord said.

God: *(Interrupting.)* Enid.

Enid: Yes, Lord?

God: I've got a job for you, too.

Enid: For me?

God: You remember those Meals With Wheels people who called...

Enid: Oh... but Lord, I can't do that. I'm a terrible...

God: Uh uh uh...

(ENID exits positively, singing the same song. Audience may applaud happily here. If another line is needed to end the play, try the following.)

God: Good. Now we might get something done around here.

© 1990 THE JOINT BOARD OF CHRISTIAN EDUCATION
The Divine Sticky Stuff: 20 short plays for churches
by Chris Chapman, Susan Chapman, Peter Gregory and Heather Allison

BIBLE READINGS

Genesis 3:1-13
Exodus 3:1-14; 4:1-15
1 Kings 19:1-5
Jonah 1:1-3

QUESTIONS FOR DISCUSSION

1. In what way and for what reason was each of the characters trying to escape from God?

2. Find out what happened to each in the end.

3. What are some of the responsibilities **we** try to avoid? How do we go about it?

4. We know deep down it isn't possible—so why do we still do it?

5. What is the best way to deal with the "Houdini complex" when you feel it coming on?

DEFEATED DEMONS

Some thoughts on *Defeated Demons*

Defeated Demons has been played to various sized audiences and has always evoked a very powerful and positive response. It is a drama which gains from a good stage atmosphere created through the characters of the demons. Costumes and makeup can be used to good effect here, but are not essential.

The demons in this drama are not to be played lightly. They are not the Seven Dwarfs. There is never any doubt that they are vicious and evil beings, and they must be played as such. Any comedy effect is derived purely from the spectacle of their total helplessness before the power of Christ's name.

The group that stages this drama should familiarise themselves with the story of the sending out of the seventy-two and, if possible, the story of the Gadarene demoniac, to see how Jesus himself dealt with demons of various sorts. Some useful references are listed below. It is also a good idea for the drama to be preceded by an on-stage reading of Luke 10:1-7, 17.

Note regarding sound and light effects

This drama in its original form had a lot of flashing light effects and sound effects of battle noises and stirring marching music with drums. These can be simulated if taped versions are not available. The most important thing is to achieve the battlefield headquarters effect with occasional outbursts of noise—such as trays of tin cans being dropped offstage, together with someone breathily going "Pup-pup-pup-pup-pup" into an offstage microphone or megaphone to sound like a machine gun. Explosions can also be done this way—but make sure it's not an expensive radio mike that's being used! Lights flashing and blackouts can be done simply by turning off the house lights. This works well if they are fluorescent tubes, but will also be effective with plain bulbs. However, the light effects are not essential here. The marching music at the end *is* essential, but can be organised easily if someone has a fairly powerful ghetto blaster with cassette tape. If the music rises in volume at the end and then is cut off as the demons run out, the effect of this drama is truly hair-raising and very powerful.

CHARACTERS:

Demon 1
Demon 2
Demon 20
Demon 31
Demon 49
Demon 68
Demon 92
Demon 106
Lucifer
Newsreader

SCENE:	*Military-style headquarters: maps, tables, etc., and if possible some sort of walkie-talkie looking thing or a telephone. DEMONS 1 and 2 are on stage. They are obviously directing a battle which can be heard occasionally in bursts of gunfire etc. from offstage (though be sure this does not mask any lines). If no curtains, then characters can enter and begin hurrying about as gunfire sounds to make it look like a battle alert scramble.*
Demon 1:	Good. There's a person about to be taken over in sector 13, reference 263948. Demon 49 is there. There's a weakening in the mind of the victim. Move in... now!
Demon 2:	*(On the move.)* Move in 49... **now!** He's in position, sir.
Demon 1:	Tell him to begin preliminary convulsions and screaming obscenities.
Demon 2:	Demon 49... screaming and obscenities commence now. Seems to be going fine, sir.
Demon 1:	Excellent. After this initial assault we'll begin tearing his family apart. Start moving in, demons 20 and 23. This is going to be fun.
	(FX: There is the sound of battle, or an explosion accompanied by flashing lights, or a general rocking about by characters on stage—grabbing tables, etc. to steady themselves.)
	Did someone knock?
Demon 2:	Was that your stomach rumbling?
Demon 1:	Not mine.
Demon 2:	Is everything still here?
Demon 1:	Yes, it's... *(Looks at map.)* No... look... number 49 is out. 20 and 23 aren't on the map. Quickly, try to contact them.
Demon 2:	Hello, hello, this is Hell operations control HQ... Demon 49, Demon 20, 23, come in... No answer. They've been cut off, sir.
Demon 1:	Where the devil... oops... I mean, where can they be?

(There are screams and DEMON 20 and DEMON 49 roll in, battered. DEMONS 1 and 2 run over to help them up.

Number 20, Number 49... where's 23?

Demon 20:	We don't know.
Demon 1:	Well, what happened to you two?
Demon 49:	I was getting settled into the mind of another victim. Things were looking good. He was wide open to my control. No defences at all. So I threw him into this great convulsion. Like this... *(Flings self on floor and writhes around.)*
Demon 20:	Yep, it was good, I saw it.
Demon 49:	*(Rising.)* Yeah.
Demon 20:	And tell them about the filthy language.
Demon 49:	Yeah. I made him start to yell out, "Ah, you silly old..."
Demon 1:	Yes yes. I've heard all that before. But what happened?
D. 20 & 49:	*(Looking at each other.)* We don't know.
Demon 49:	There was a blinding flash of light.
Demon 20:	And a burst of sound like angels singing and shouting.
Demon 2:	Yuk! It must have been awful.
Demon 49:	It was. Next thing I know, I'm out of the victim and flying through the air head first. Went straight through a wall, over the city dump and landed here.
Demon 20:	Me too. I was just about to move in with 23 on the victim's family members and then... whammo! I landed here. I think 23 just got blasted. Last time I saw him he was riding on the back of a big pig, heading down a hill towards a lake. Never saw him again.
Demon 1:	Scratch Number 23. He must have done a kamikaze.
Demon 2:	So what's causing all this trouble?
Demon 49:	I don't know. Never seen anything like it.
Demon 20:	Ridiculous. Perhaps it was an earthquake.
Demon 1:	Look here, you two—you've botched up a perfectly good mission. Now get out there and get back into that victim and wreck him. Home, family, career, everything.
Demon 2:	And you, 20. Get the dumbness out. We haven't used that for a while. Make them so they can't speak a word.
Demon 1:	And 49... forget convulsions and blasphemies. Make it violence, okay? I want that victim hurting other people too.
Demon 49:	Got it.
Demon 1:	Now get out there to sector 13.

D. 20 & 49:	**Charge!** *(They both rush off.)*
Demon 1:	There, that's better.
	(Offstage screams. DEMONS 20 and 49 stagger back on.)
Demon 49:	Oh, my head...
Demon 20:	I'm seeing double.
Demon 1:	*(In exclamation.)* Good heavens! *(Everyone hisses.)* I mean... what happened?
Demon 49:	I just head-butted the victim to try and get him back in. It was like running into concrete.
Demon 20:	There's some sort of coating around them. We can't get through.
	(FX: Short battle sounds. DEMONS 92 and 106 roll in.)
Demon 106:	Demons 106 and 92 reporting back, sir.
Demon 92:	Can we take a break now?
Demon 1:	What happened to you two?
Demon 106:	It was the most awful experience of my whole eternity. There I was, nicely settled into my victim. Been there for years... and all that time he'd been a total reprobate. I'd had him in brawls, drinking to excess, committing crimes... all the good stuff. Then this other bloke comes along. I was about to make my victim smash his face in when the other bloke says a few words. **Bang!** I woke up here.
Demon 92:	Same here. I got chucked out the same way.
	(FX: More battle noises. DEMONS 31 and 68 roll in.)
Demon 2:	This is ridiculous. Not more! Where have you come from?
Demon 68:	The red light district.
Demon 31:	Sector 19.
Demon 68:	We got thrown out.
Demon 31:	There's these guys getting around who are throwing us out.
Demon 2:	Can't you beat them up or something?
Demon 31:	No! They've got... the **name**!
All:	Aghhh!
Demon 49:	Yes... it's all coming back to me.
Demon 20:	Don't mention the **name**!
Demon 31:	That name. It's horrible.
Demon 1:	What name?
Demon 31:	The name of...
All:	**Nooo!** *(DEMON 68 claps hand over 31's mouth.)*

Demon 31: Gee, thanks. I forgot I wasn't supposed to say the name of Jesus Christ.

(FX: A huge explosion, plus as much rocking round, table upsetting, light flashing and tin can dropping as can be achieved.)

Demon 68: *(Getting up groggily.)* Don't ever say that name again.

Demon 31: Sorry.

Demon 1: So this is what's causing the problem?

Demon 49: Yes, it's that name. That awful name.

Demon 68: They use it all the time.

Demon 92: Seventy-two of them.

Demon 106: They've all got the name.

Demon 92: And there's nothing we can do about it.

Demon 106: All they've got to do is say, "Get out in the name of..." *(All gasp and flinch.)* ...you know who." And we're finished.

Demon 1: *(Pacing up and down.)* But there must be some way of defeating the power of that name.

Demon 2: There must be some way to neutralise it.

Demon 49: Well, we can't.

Demon 20: No way.

Demon 106: I don't want to go back out there.

Demon 92: I want a job down here. I don't want to be a missionary.

Demon 31: Give me a job shovelling coals in the deepest pit we have. I don't care how deep.

Demon 68: Just don't send us out there again.

(General wailing from all.)

Demon 1: *(To DEMON 2.)* This is ridiculous.

Demon 2: They're completely demoralised.

Demon 1: They're on the point of mutiny.

Demon 2: Utter defeatism.

Demon 1: *(To the rest.)* Look, you have to pull yourselves together.

Demon 68: It's no use. We're helpless against this new power.

Demon 1: Then there's only one person who can deal with this sort of fire power.

Demon 2: We've got to cut the red tape and go straight to the... *(Points up, then realises his mistake and points down.)* ... bottom.

Demon 49: You mean...

Demon 1: Big "L".

All:	Oooh!
Demon 1:	31, go down to the lower levels and tell Big L we need help.
Demon 31:	Who?
Demon 1:	Big L. Tell him it's urgent.
Demon 31:	Right. *(Hesitates.)* Who's Big L?
Demon 2:	L! Lucifer, you fool!
Demon 31:	Oh... the boss.
	(Exit DEMON 31. There may be a suitable sound of rumbling or a bit of smoke for the entry of LUCIFER. Some talcum powder thrown in ahead of him from offstage will do the job.)
Lucifer:	*(Enters grandly as others fawn around him.)* Well, what is it?
Demon 1:	Sir, we seem to have a problem.
Lucifer:	What sort of problem?
Demon 2:	The opposition, sir. They've got a new weapon. We've never come across it before.
Lucifer:	Well, what is this new weapon? Come on, spit it out. You interrupted me in the middle of planning another war, with starvation and disease.
Demon 1:	Sir, it's a new name. The Son of God. He's come. He's spreading his powerful name everywhere.
Demon 2:	His disciples are using it to chuck us out—left, right and centre. We can't defend ourselves.
Demon 1:	We try to fight, but we haven't got a hope in... here.
Lucifer:	Useless fools. Imbeciles! *(They cower.)* You need some **real** power. I'll show you what needs to be done. Get out of my way, you pathetic peasants. Just leave it to me. *(Stalks out in disgust, kicking DEMONS out of the way.)*
Demon 1:	He'll handle it.
Demon 2:	When he gets hold of that lot, he'll make mince meat of them.
All:	Yeah!
Demon 49:	I wonder what he'll do.
Demon 20:	I reckon he'll massacre them with some of the top line demons.
Demon 68:	He'll take on the Son of God himself.
Demon 31:	But it won't be the soft sell this time.
Demon 92:	Not like the forty days in the wilderness.
Demon 106:	This time it will be for real.
Newsreader:	*(Can be voice over, or can actually come on stage and do the quick news flash—then exit with a worried look at surrounding DEMONS.)* Here is a late newsflash from the worldwide sources of the Hades Herald. Earlier today the Son of

God was sentenced to death and crucified, after being handed over to the authorities through the assistance of one of his own followers.

All: Yeah! He did it! *(General celebration.)*

Demon 49: Big L did it. I knew he would.

Demon 20: Crucifixion. What a way to go!

Demon 68: And get that bit about being betrayed.

Demon 31: Yeah. By one of his own followers.

Demon 92: Nice touch, Big L. What a great system.

Demon 106: Pulled the rug right out from under his feet.

Demon 1: Now we'll be able to regain our lost territory.

Demon 2: We'll launch the greatest demonic attack the world has ever seen.

Demon 1: Come on, you lot. Let's look at the map.

(They cluster around. Unnoticed by them, LUCIFER enters. They see him and mob him to offer congratulations, but he is obviously uncertain and flustered. In the end he explodes.)

Lucifer: Stop! Shut up!

Demon 1: What's wrong, boss? You did a great job.

Demon 2: You killed him.

Demon 1: Put him away.

Lucifer: But that was three days ago.

Demon 2: So?

Lucifer: He's **back**!

(There is stunned silence.)

Demon 1: What?

Lucifer: I said he's back. What do you want me to do—say it a thousand times? I thought he was dead... but now he's back.

Demon 1: *(Trying to help.)* But boss, we'll mob him. He's only one Son of God. He can't beat all of us.

Lucifer: Fools. Don't you understand? I mean—he's back and he's not alone.

All: What?

Lucifer: He's got an army of them. The Holy Spirit is here too.

Demon: Oh no, not him!

Lucifer: And he's creating a whole army of Christian soldiers.

Demon 1: What?

Lucifer:	There's hundreds of them. The Holy Spirit is getting into their hearts and lives. They're full of power. It's the end... for all of us.
All:	Oh no!
Lucifer:	*(Shouting above the panic.)* Listen!

(They stop and cluster together, trembling and listening. There is quiet... and then, very faintly, can be heard the sounds of either triumphal, gutsy hymn singing, or marching feet, or military music or drums, or a couple of these combined. Lights begin to fade ever so slowly as the sound grows stronger. This is when the hair on the audience begins to rise.)

Demon 1:	But what does it mean?

(Music grows louder.)

Lucifer:	It means he's coming. *(Music louder.)* They're **all** coming!

(DEMONS cluster around LUCIFER as music grows ever louder to a peak. At that point the DEMONS can run screaming in panic into the audience and out, or offstage, and the music can be cut. Or music and lights can be cut simultaneously, leaving the audience with a mental picture of the defeated demons clustering in terror around their equally terrified master.)

BIBLE READINGS

Luke 10:1-17
Luke 9:37-45
Acts 8:9-24
1 Kings 19:9-13

QUESTIONS FOR DISCUSSION

1. Read Luke 10:1-17. Why do you think the seventy-two returned "with joy"? What other feelings might they have had?

2. How has Jesus defeated Satan once and for all?

3. Read Luke 9:37-45. List some other New Testament examples where the power of Jesus' name and word were able to counter demonic power.

4. It is easy to see how, to some, the name of Jesus has become like a magic incantation to be used for their own glorification to try to achieve "magic" effects. What are the dangers and shortcomings of this attitude?

5. How can God's power help us in our own daily lives?

6. God's power does not always work in the spectacular or loudly miraculous. What are the quiet ways in which this power comes to us? Sometimes the power may even seem powerless until we realise God's plan—discuss this idea.